Vegetarian Slimming wo̶... ...
to do, slimming the veg... ...
choose from a vast rang͟ͅ ͟ͅᴏf delicious recipes and
shows you how to think health. Rose Elliot's
Vegetarian Slimming includes over 100 imaginative and
mouthwatering recipes for starters, main courses,
snacks, puddings, dinner parties and choices for
vegans, and is packed with advice on nutrition,
exercise, meditation and relaxation – everything you
need for a healthier lifestyle. You will be slimmer *and*
healthier – and stay that way.

Rose Elliot is one of Britain's top cookery writers. She has been a vegetarian since the age of three and was the first cookery writer to show that vegetarian food can be 'Simply Delicious' and 'Not Just a Load of Old Lentils'. She is married with three daughters and lives in London and Hampshire.

ALSO BY ROSE ELLIOT

Not Just a Load of Old Lentils
The Bean Book
Beanfeast
Gourmet Vegetarian Cooking
Your Very Good Health
Vegetarian Dishes of the World
Rose Elliot's Mother and Baby Book
The Complete Vegetarian Cookbook
Cheap and Easy
The New Simply Delicious
Vegetarian Cookery
The Zodiac Cookbook
The New Vegetarian Cookbook
The Supreme Vegetarian Cookbook
Rose Elliot's Vegetarian Christmas

VEGETARIAN SLIMMING

Rose Elliot

ORION

An Orion paperback
First published in Great Britain by Chapmans Publishers Ltd in 1991.
This paperback edition published in 1994 by Orion Books Ltd,
Orion House, 5 Upper St Martin's Lane, London WC2H 9EA

A CIP catalogue record for this book is
available from the British Library.

ISBN: 1 85797 504 9

Printed in England by Clays Ltd, St Ives plc

To my beloved parents, who started it all,
with deepest love and thanks

Contents

Acknowledgements

I'd like to thank everyone who has been involved in the production of this book, particularly Ian and Marjory Chapman, David North and Greg Hill for their enthusiasm for the project. My thanks to Kelly Davis for her inspired editing and to Yvonne Holland for her hard work on the manuscript; to my agent Barbara Levy for her help and supportiveness; to my family for their love and their patience, and especially to my husband Anthony for giving me so much help with the manuscript, notably with the Calories and the sections on the psychological aspects of slimming. I am also most grateful to those experts who have generously shared their knowledge with me and kindly read and made helpful comments on the relevant sections of this book. To Doris Grant, leading exponent of the Hay System, for help with the Food-Combining section; to Lilian Verner Bonds, Colour Therapist; to John Ramsell, Trustee and Curator of Bach Flower Remedies; and to Jenny Beeken, teacher of the Iyengar system of Yoga.

Notes

~⊰⊱~

ABOUT CALORIES

The energy value of a food is the amount of energy our
bodies can extract from it by combining it with oxygen.
This value is expressed in Calories or kilocalories (kcals)
which are units for measuring heat. As the efficiency of the
conversion process varies for each person the Calories are
guides, not absolute quantities. The large Calorie used in
nutrition is 1000 times the old calorie (cgs).
1 Calorie = 1 kcal = 1000 calories
1 calorie = 4.184 joules (J) or 0.004184 kilojoules (kJ)
1 Calorie or 1 kcal = 4.184 kJ
Because of the confusion of names there is now a move to
use kilojoules (kJ) rather than Calories.

METRIC AND IMPERIAL WEIGHTS

Recipes are given in both metric and Imperial weights.
Use either, but it's best to keep to one or the other within
a recipe. All spoon measurements are level unless stated
otherwise: teaspoons are 5 ml and tablespoons are 15 ml.

Readers in Australia and New Zealand, please note that
the standard Australian tablespoon measurement is
20 ml.

SYMBOLS USED IN THE MENUS AND RECIPES

Throughout the book these symbols indicate which recipes, menus and their variations are suitable for vegans, hip and thigh dieters and food-combiners.

Ⓥ for vegan

Ⓟ for protein

Ⓒ for carbohydrate

ⒻⓋ for fruit and vegetable

Ⓝ for neutral

ⒽⓉ for hip and thigh dieters

HEALTH NOTE

The Vegetarian Slimming Plan is a highly effective, healthy way to get slim and stay slim. However, as with any diet, it is always wise to ask your doctor's advice before starting if you are in any doubt about your health.

Introduction

WHY CHOOSE A VEGETARIAN DIET?

Having bought this book, you've obviously decided to go on a diet. But why choose the Vegetarian Slimming Plan? Whether you've been vegetarian or vegan for many years, or you just want to give up meat for a while, there are plenty of good reasons to go for this particular method of losing weight. A vegetarian diet is best for slimming and health because it:

- **Cuts out one major source of Calories and saturated fat – meat**

In a normal diet, over a quarter of all the fat comes from meat. Even meat which looks lean contains considerable amounts of hidden fat. Eating less saturated fat reduces your risk of heart disease and strokes.

- **Contains plenty of fresh fruit and vegetables**

Fresh fruit and vegetables are rich in vitamins and minerals. In addition, there is increasing evidence to show that eating 450 g/1 lb of fresh fruit and vegetables each day protects against certain forms of cancer, particularly those of the cervix and the lung.

- **Is naturally high in fibre**

Fibre fills you up and helps stave off hunger, as well as being essential for general health. Many modern diseases have been linked with eating too little fibre. These include constipation, diverticular disease, haemorrhoids, hiatus hernia, appendicitis and cancer of the colon.

- **Reduces the risk of infection from diseases**

Meat is more likely to contain harmful bacteria and organisms than vegetable produce. Despite all the precautions taken in abattoirs, and the meat industry generally, there is still a risk of infection. Many people are particularly worried about the possibility of BSE ('mad cow disease') being passed on to humans.

In addition, when you choose to slim on a vegetarian diet, you make a positive contribution to the health of the planet. You help to:

- **Slow down the destruction of the rainforests**

One of the reasons why these are being cut down is to grow cheap grain to fatten beef for consumption in the USA and Europe.

- **Make the world's food go round**

It takes 16 lb of grain and soya to produce 1 lb of beef. This is a very inefficient use of the world's resources. That amount of grain and soya would feed an African family for a whole week.

- **Save water**

It takes 11,365 litres/2500 gallons of water – as much as a typical family uses for all purposes in a month – to produce 450 g/1 lb of beef.

- **Save energy**
- **Cut down on pollution**

One cow produces as much waste each day as 16 humans, polluting the rivers with harmful nitrates and the atmosphere with methane.

14

• **Reduce the suffering of animals**
This applies particularly to animals being reared intensively in cramped and inhumane conditions.

So, considering all these factors, slimming on a vegetarian diet makes a great deal of sense. Indeed, some people find that they lose weight naturally when they stop eating meat. However, when you decide to slim I think you want to be sure of a steady weight-loss. That is why, in addition to being vegetarian, this book offers a diet based on the reliable Calorie system. For those who prefer not to count Calories, a simple food-combining diet is provided as a healthy and pleasant alternative.

TO COUNT OR NOT TO COUNT CALORIES?

Calories (also known as kilocalories) express the amount of energy that we can extract from food by combining it with oxygen. If we take in more food, more Calories than we need, most of this extra energy is stored in the form of fat, for future use, and we put on weight. This is a natural safeguard to enable us to lay down food in times of surplus for use in times of shortage. Nowadays most of us have a regular supply of food and we no longer need this survival mechanism. If we take in the same number of Calories as we use (approximately 2200 Calories for a woman, 2600 or more for a man, depending on how active we are), our weight stays fairly level. And if we take in fewer Calories than our body needs, our body draws on its fat supplies for fuel and we lose weight. Food-combining is a way of reducing Calories by eating foods only in certain combinations.

15

So, in theory, all we need to do if we are overweight is to reduce the number of Calories we are taking in or take care to eat the right foods, and the weight will drop off. However, as anyone who has ever tried to lose weight knows, it's not as easy as it sounds. Dieting doesn't only concern the physical body; our minds, senses and emotions are also involved, and can make weight-loss more or less likely to happen. For instance, although you may think you want to lose weight, and tell yourself all the good reasons for doing so, if you are not truly happy about losing it, you can go on diet after diet, but you won't succeed. You may keep to a diet for a while and get slim, and then put all the weight back on again, so that life becomes a constant struggle to keep the pounds at bay. Or you may try to use mental willpower to impose on yourself a diet which doesn't suit your tastes, personality or lifestyle, but you probably won't be able to keep to it for long.

WHAT'S DIFFERENT ABOUT THIS DIET?

In order to lose weight successfully, and to keep it off, you need to understand the emotions which influence your choice of foods and your ability to lose weight, so that you can work with them instead of against them. You need a diet which pleases your senses and fits in with your lifestyle. And you need a healthy diet, which, combined with exercise, will keep your body in peak condition. But above all, you need to really want to succeed – for you. And then you have to be prepared to put this 'will to succeed' into action.

The Vegetarian Slimming Plan offers you this holistic approach to slimming. It aims to get your body, senses, mind and emotions working harmoniously together to make you slim and healthy, to create the body you have always wanted, and to keep it that way.

Part 1
Successful Slimming

As I've said, in order to lose weight successfully, and to stay that way, you need really to want to get slim – for *you*. Not because it would please someone else, or someone else has told you that you should slim, but because *you* want to have a slim, lithe, healthy body. The next step is to be honest: to look at yourself clearly, weigh yourself, and work out how much weight you need to lose. Then think about what you're doing now, to see what's causing you to gain weight: notice your eating habits, and the triggers which prompt you to eat. This will enable you to plan a diet which feels harmonious to you and fits in with your lifestyle. Finally, it's important to set yourself a target amount of weight to lose, and make a commitment to yourself that you *will* do so.

BE HONEST

It's not always easy to see ourselves clearly and to face up to the fact that we need to lose weight. We can kid ourselves that we've got big bones or a sluggish metabolism and we can wear loose clothes to cover up the fat. But this doesn't help in the long run. We need to take off the blinkers and view ourselves objectively.

I think it is very helpful to look at yourself without any clothes on in a full-length mirror, or preferably two mirrors so that you can see yourself from all angles! Try to be objective and dispassionate. If you are not happy with what you see, don't criticise and condemn yourself. The person in the mirror is the starting point for the new slim you; and looking at yourself honestly and lovingly is the first step towards your goal.

WEIGH YOURSELF

The scales will also give you an unbiased verdict on whether or not you need to lose weight. So, see what you weigh, and compare this with the weights given in the tables on pages 21 and 22. (Bear in mind that normal bathroom scales may not be absolutely accurate. Make sure that they are properly adjusted, and if the scales are on a carpet, try putting a piece of hardboard underneath them so that they are standing on a flat, hard surface.)

The weight tables are based on the 'ideal weight' tables used by insurance companies. These are calculated by taking the weights at which the fewest people suffer from disease. Anyone who weighs more than this has a greater risk of suffering from disease, and the more overweight they are, the greater the risk.

The tables give the recommended weights for men and women according to height. Maximum and minimum recommended weights are given; your ideal weight will probably be somewhere in between the two. Only you can decide this. It may be the weight at which you have felt

If you are a man

Height		Minimum		Average		Maximum	
1.57m	5ft 2in	51.0kg	8st 0lb	55.5kg	8st 11lb	64.0kg	10st 1lb
1.60m	5ft 3in	52.0kg	8st 3lb	57.5kg	9st 1lb	65.0kg	10st 4lb
1.63m	5ft 4in	53.0kg	8st 5lb	59.0kg	9st 4lb	67.0kg	10st 8lb
1.65m	5ft 5in	54.5kg	8st 9lb	60.0kg	9st 7lb	69.0kg	10st 12lb
1.68m	5ft 6in	56.0kg	8st 12lb	61.5kg	9st 10lb	70.5kg	11st 1lb
1.70m	5ft 7in	58.0kg	9st 2lb	63.5kg	10st 0lb	73.5kg	11st 7lb
1.73m	5ft 8in	59.5kg	9st 5lb	65.5kg	10st 5lb	75.5kg	11st 12lb
1.75m	5ft 9in	61.5kg	9st 10lb	67.5kg	10st 9lb	77.0kg	12st 1lb
1.78m	5ft 10in	63.5kg	10st 0lb	69.5kg	10st 13lb	79.0kg	12st 5lb
1.80m	5ft 11in	65.0kg	10st 4lb	71.5kg	11st 4lb	81.0kg	12st 11lb
1.83m	6ft 0in	67.0kg	10st 8lb	73.5kg	11st 8lb	83.5kg	13st 2lb
1.85m	6ft 1in	69.0kg	10st 12lb	75.0kg	11st 12lb	85.5kg	13st 7lb
1.88m	6ft 2in	71.0kg	11st 2lb	77.5kg	12st 3lb	88.0kg	13st 12lb
1.90m	6ft 3in	72.5kg	11st 3lb	79.5kg	12st 8lb	90.5kg	14st 3lb

If you are a woman

Height		Minimum		Average		Maximum	
1.47m	4ft 10in	41.5kg	6st 8lb	46.0kg	7st 4lb	52.5kg	8st 4lb
1.50m	4ft 11in	42.5kg	6st 10lb	47.0kg	7st 6lb	55.0kg	8st 10lb
1.52m	5ft 0in	43.5kg	6st 12lb	48.5kg	7st 9lb	56.5kg	8st 13lb
1.55m	5ft 1in	45.0kg	7st 1lb	50.0kg	7st 12lb	57.0kg	9st 2lb
1.57m	5ft 2in	46.0kg	7st 4lb	51.0kg	8st 1lb	59.5kg	9st 5lb
1.60m	5ft 3in	47.5kg	7st 7lb	52.5kg	8st 4lb	60.5kg	9st 8lb
1.63m	5ft 4in	49.5kg	7st 10lb	54.5kg	8st 8lb	62.5kg	9st 12lb
1.65m	5ft 5in	50.0kg	7st 13lb	55.5kg	8st 11lb	64.5kg	10st 2lb
1.68m	5ft 6in	51.5kg	8st 2lb	58.0kg	9st 2lb	66.0kg	10st 6lb
1.70m	5ft 7in	53.5kg	8st 6lb	59.5kg	9st 6lb	68.0kg	10st 10lb
1.73m	5ft 8in	55.0kg	8st 10lb	61.5kg	9st 10lb	70.0kg	11st 0lb
1.75m	5ft 9in	57.0kg	9st 0lb	63.5kg	10st 0lb	71.5kg	11st 3lb
1.78m	5ft 10in	59.0kg	9st 4lb	65.0kg	10st 4lb	74.0kg	11st 9lb
1.80m	5ft 11in	60.5kg	9st 8lb	67.0kg	10st 8lb	76.0kg	12st 0lb
1.83m	6ft 0in	62.5kg	9st 12lb	69.0kg	10st 12lb	78.5kg	12st 5lb

and looked your best in the past. If you are not sure, set a target weight suitable for your height, using the table, and then, as you approach that weight, be guided by how your body feels; you can choose to stop, or you can go on and see how you feel when you have lost another pound or two. Make a note of your target weight and subtract it from your present weight to find out how much you need to lose.

IDEAL WEIGHT TABLES

Height should be measured without shoes. Weights should be measured without clothing, but if you do weigh yourself with clothes on, allow about 1.5 kg/3 lb extra.

LOOK AT WHAT YOU'RE DOING NOW

As we have seen, if you are overweight, you are either taking in now, or have in the past taken in, more Calories than you have used up. In order to take off — and keep off — this extra weight, you need to find out where the extra Calories are coming from, and when. This will help you to find a diet which fits your lifestyle, and also to understand any emotional issues which might be influencing your eating habits and encouraging you to put on weight.

A good way of doing this is to keep a record of everything you eat and drink. For 2 to 3 days, write down the time and place where you ate (and/or drank), who you were with, what you were doing and how you were feeling. (See the example over page.) You don't need to

SAMPLE DAY'S RECORD

Day	Time	Place	Company	Mood	Hungry?	Food eaten	Activity
monday	8.00	kitchen	alone	sleepy	no	coffee 1 piece of toast	getting ready for work
	10.30	work	with colleagues	lively	no	coffee 1 biscuit	working at desk
	1.00	work	colleagues	?	yes	cheese bap apple	chatting
	3.30	work	colleagues	busy	no	cup of tea	working at desk
	6.30	home	family	harassed	yes	pizza baked potato salad	sitting in front of television

put in the Calorie values of the food. The important thing is to see what pattern emerges. Alternatively, if you don't want to keep a record, just think carefully about your eating habits. In either case, aim to answer the questions below. Try not to criticise yourself as you do so, or feel any sense of blame or judgement. Just stand aside from your emotions and look at yourself and the foods that you eat as if you were an impartial observer.

WHEN, WHY AND WHAT DO YOU EAT?

Pattern of meals
1   Are you eating three regular meals a day, or do you skip breakfast and lunch and then eat a lot in the evening?

Snacks
2   Do you find it difficult to resist snacks? Do you nibble food without thinking?

Drinks
3   How many cups of tea and coffee (or other milky beverages) do you drink each day?
4   How many sweet or alcoholic drinks do you have?

Fatty foods
5   Is your diet high in fatty foods? See page 31.

Changes in eating habits
6   If you have recently started to gain weight, have you

changed your diet in some way? Or are you eating the same but getting less exercise?

Quantity
7   Do you simply eat too much – or find it difficult to stop?

Emotional needs
8   Do you have a 'gnawing' feeling after meals, even though you know you can't be hungry?
9   Are you very strong-willed all day – or for several days, or weeks – and then, suddenly, find that your self-control breaks down and you 'binge'?
10   Do you eat because you are bored/stressed/angry/unhappy?

Let's look at these issues in more detail.

1   Do you skip breakfast and lunch and then eat a lot in the evening?
This is a very common pattern in people who are over-weight. Although it may work for some people, it has a number of disadvantages. It means that the body is going for a long period – from one evening until the next – without fuel. And this period includes most of the day, when much energy is used. Starting the day on an empty stomach – after the natural 'fast' of the night – has been shown to lead to reduced concentration and learning ability, slower reactions and greater risk of accidents. Levels of cholesterol and triglycerides (harmful fats) in our blood tend to rise when we eat less than three meals a day. This in turn increases our risk of heart disease. So, from a physical point of view, eating three regular meals a day would seem to be a good idea.

Having three regular meals a day can also be helpful

psychologically. When we eat again after skipping meals, we often feel that we deserve a reward for our self-discipline and we tend to eat much more as a result. Also, in the evening our self-control is at its lowest. So eating nothing all day may lead to eating more in the long run. This 'fasting/feasting' syndrome is one of the characteristics of the binge-eater, and leads to a tendency for eating to get out of control. This is why one of the rules of Weight Watchers is that dieters do not skip meals.

Another good reason to get into the habit of eating three regular meals a day is that when you allow yourself to have breakfast and lunch as well as an evening meal you establish a sense of harmony and a feeling of being nourished rather than deprived. Indeed, for some people, simply getting into the habit of eating three regular low-fat, low-sugar meals, and limiting snacks (see page 28) can be enough to start the pounds rolling off. Of course you can vary the exact timing of these meals to suit yourself. In general, slimmers are advised to eat fairly early in the evening but you might find, as I do, that it's more helpful to have a late meal, which you can look forward to. I find that if I eat too early, I end up wanting to nibble later.

However, whilst three regular meals a day may be sound and sensible, it may not be right for you. For instance, some people prefer to eat very lightly – perhaps just fruit – during the day and then to have a large evening meal. Again, other people like to have several small snack meals during the day instead of three 'proper' meals. Both these systems can work well. The most important thing is to work *with* your preferences rather than going against them, if you want to keep to a diet. The Vegetarian Slimming Plan is based on three meals a day, although you can time these to suit yourself. You can also break them up into several smaller snacks, or you can 'save' some

Calories from earlier in the day to allow for a larger evening meal if you wish.

2 Do you find it difficult to resist snacks? Do you nibble food without thinking?

It's surprising how many extra Calories you can eat in silly ways, without even thinking about it: that honey spoon you lick before you wash it up, the crusts you cut off the children's sandwiches and eat, the food you taste as you're cooking, the broken biscuit you eat when you're putting them away in the tin. All these Calories add up, yet you probably hardly notice you've eaten them. You certainly haven't *really* enjoyed them. So resolve, from now on, to notice what you are eating, and to make every Calorie count. Make every Calorie you eat a Calorie you really enjoy!

When it comes to eating actual snacks, these are fine if they are counted as meals, and eating several snacks a day can be a good way of losing weight. But the trouble with snacks is that they are usually eaten *as well as*, not instead of meals; and most snack foods contain a large proportion of fat and/or sugar, and are thus high in Calories. For instance, a small packet of crisps contains 150 Calories – even the low-fat ones are 125; a chocolate biscuit is 125 Calories; a handful of salted nuts is 170 Calories; a small bar of chocolate, a Danish pastry or a jam doughnut are 250–300 Calories.

The other problem with these snacks is that once you start eating them, it's difficult to stop. If you have several of these in a day, it's easy to see how you can soon notch up 500, 600, or more, Calories. That could be a quarter of your normal day's Calories or half your Calorie allowance if you're slimming on 1000–1200 Calories a day. If you really love snack foods, eat them, but *plan* for them in your diet; save some Calories to allow you to have your favourite snack. For more about this, see Varying the Diet, on page 79. The funny thing is that you may well find that you lose the taste for these snacks as your diet progresses.

3 How many cups of tea and coffee (or other milky beverages) do you drink each day?

Whilst tea and coffee themselves contain no Calories to speak of, as soon as you add milk and/or sugar the Calories mount up, and this can add a surprising number of Calories to your daily total. Cups of tea and coffee can be very helpful when you're slimming, giving the comfort of something warm and taking the edge off hunger pangs, but you do need to allow for the Calories unless you are taking them black. Full-fat milk is 40 Calories for 50 ml/2 fl oz, while sugar is around 20 Calories a teaspoonful: a hefty 60 Calories a cup! You can reduce the Calories by using skimmed milk, which is 20 Calories for 50 ml/2 fl oz, and cutting out sugar or using artificial sweetener. And if you take your beverages black, the Calories are reduced to 0.

Other beverages, such as hot chocolate, do contain Calories, so these have to be added on to the Calories in the milk and sugar. Drinking chocolate, for instance, is 35 Calories for 2 teaspoons, and malted milk powder is 35 Calories for 1 teaspoon (an average serving). You would probably use more than the suggested 50 ml/2 fl oz of milk to make these, too. That does not mean you can't have a soothing milky drink and still lose weight; but you need to be aware that you could be notching up 100 or more Calories in doing so, and allow for this when planning your day's meals.

4 How many sweet or alcoholic drinks do you have?

Soft drinks and alcoholic drinks are both high in Calories. A 300 ml/½ pint glass of cola drink, for instance, is 110

Calories, and lemonade is 60 Calories for the same amount. Of course slimline versions of these drinks contain hardly any Calories, and switching to these and to slimline mixer drinks makes good sense. Still or sparkling bottled water, with a sliver of lemon or lime, is Calorie-free, and more health-giving and cleansing than any slimline drinks. Freshly squeezed lemon or lime juice topped up with chilled water, and sweetened (if you like) with artificial sweetener, can also be considered Calorie-free. Like tea and coffee, these drinks can fill you up in a most helpful way when you're slimming, but make sure you're drinking the low-Calorie versions.

Alcoholic drinks, too, are a great way of sending your day's Calorie total sky-high! Wine is around 100 Calories a glass, a glass of sherry 70–80 Calories; beer, lager and cider, around 100 Calories for 300 ml/½ pint. (For more information on the Calories in alcoholic drinks, see Can You Drink and Diet? page 112.) Just a couple of pints of beer will notch up around 400 Calories, and low-alcohol versions, if you like them, are a little, but not much better. Low-Calorie wines are about 40 Calories per 142 ml glass; low-Calorie beers and lagers about 54 Calories for 300 ml/½ pint.

If soft or alcoholic drinks are running away with your Calories, you may only need to cut back on these in order to lose weight. In doing so, you can make it easier by not putting yourself in the way of temptation. If there are certain places or situations where you know it will be difficult for you not to drink, either avoid or cut down on them; or decide beforehand to stick to just one drink (or slimline tonic) and pass on the peanuts and crisps. Ordering a bottle of spring water and drinking this alongside an alcoholic drink (or continuing to top up the drink with spring water) can also help.

5 Is your diet high in fatty foods?

Fried foods, meat, full-fat milk, cream, cheese, chocolate, mayonnaise and oily salad dressings, gravies and sauces, eggs, chips, crisps, nuts, cakes, biscuits, chocolate, ice-cream, avocado pears, butter and margarine are all high in fat. Fat has more than double the number of Calories per gram that protein and carbohydrate have; and, in addition, the body stores extra Calories of fat more readily than it stores extra Calories of protein and carbohydrate. So, not only do the Calories mount up more quickly if you are eating many fatty foods, but your body is inclined to store the surplus! And, of course, too much fat is unhealthy.

Simply reducing the number of fatty foods you eat can cut Calories considerably. You could also try grilling, instead of frying food, and choosing reduced-fat versions where possible, such as skimmed milk and reduced-fat cheese instead of the full-fat types; and low-fat spread instead of butter or margarine. This seems to be a particularly effective way of reducing weight in hips and thighs. See the Vegetarian Hip and Thigh Diet page 152.

6 If you have recently started to gain weight, have you changed your diet in some way? Or are you eating the same but getting less exercise?

Quite small changes in your diet can, over a period of time, make a difference to your weight. So if your weight has crept up, and you can trace this to a simple change in your eating habits, correcting this, and cutting back a little in addition, will help you to lose the weight. One lady realised that it was since she'd started having a glass of sherry each evening that she had gradually put on weight. She gave up the sherry and also changed from full-fat milk to skimmed milk and the pounds dropped off. In the same way, simply swapping full-fat milk with skimmed milk or soya milk and giving up sugar in tea and coffee (or using artificial sweeteners instead of sugar) can have a similar effect.

Of course if these extras are the result of a change in lifestyle, involving more 'social' eating and drinking, the problem may be more difficult to tackle, but it can still be done. (See Eating Out, pages 106 and 145.)

Although most exercise does not burn up great quantities of Calories – 15 minutes of fast walking only burns up about 80 Calories – the amount of exercise you take can also have a slow but sure effect on your weight. If you can attribute your extra weight to taking less exercise, simply taking more exercise again could do the trick. (One man dated his extra 3 kg/7 lb back to six months before, when he'd stopped taking his dog for walks twice a day.) Consider some of the ways of fitting more exercise into your daily routine. This can be done in simple ways such as walking instead of driving to the shops, getting off the bus one or two stops earlier than usual, or cycling to work instead of driving. For more about this, and other forms of exercise, see page 45.

Perhaps, however, you have a medical complaint which makes you less able to exercise now? In this case, do consult your doctor. A small reduction in your Calorie intake may be necessary if you cannot exercise sufficiently to burn up the extra Calories. Or perhaps a combination of modest exercise and a lower Calorie intake might be the best solution. It follows that the way to lose weight is either to take in fewer Calories than you need, or to take more exercise so that your body burns up more Calories. Taking in fewer Calories will result in a steady loss of weight; getting more exercise without changing your diet may result in weight-loss over several months, but it will be slow. Exercise certainly increases your fitness and feeling of well-being, however.

7   Do you simply eat too much – or find it difficult to stop?

You may find that, although you can be very self-disciplined, there are some occasions, such as in the evening, or when you are bored or stressed, when you simply eat too much. Having three regular meals a day, as explained above, might help this. And if you go on a slimming diet, you will also find that it is a problem which becomes easier to cope with. As we eat less, we want less. So, although it takes a great deal of self-discipline at the beginning of a diet, it does usually get easier.

Eating less will gradually become so natural that you won't have to think about it. To start with, though, it is helpful to plan your life so as to make it as easy as possible to get into new, slimming habits. In fact making life easy for yourself generally – being kind to yourself – is a very important aspect of successful slimming. I have explained this in greater detail on pages 262–265. See also page 43 for ways in which you can make it easier to eat in a 'slimming' way at mealtimes.

Sometimes, particularly when you start a slimming diet, it's difficult to tell when you've had enough to eat. This *does* get easier. One way of helping yourself is to eat more slowly. This will make you think you've eaten more than you have! And having some pleasant activity planned for after you have eaten can help, too.

8   Do you have a 'gnawing' feeling after meals, even though you know you can't be hungry?

This may be due to boredom, frustration or tension: see page 35. The relaxation technique on page 270 might be helpful, too. Or it may be that you have chosen over-processed foods which lack fibre and real goodness. Eat the 'whole' version of foods – wholemeal bread, wholegrain cereals, brown rice, baked potatoes in their skins, with small quantities of fat (which helps to stave off hunger pangs), together with plenty of fresh fruit and vegetables, and see if this helps. The meals in the Vegetarian Slimming Plan are based on these types of food and should therefore prove satisfying.

9 Are you very strong-willed all day – or for several days, or weeks – and then, suddenly, find that your self-control breaks down and you 'binge'?

Binge-eating is when we eat and eat and are unable to stop. We may well have been extremely strong-willed all day – or for several days, or weeks – and then, suddenly, our self-control breaks down and we start to gorge ourselves without control. This leads to a terrible feeling of being bloated, and of great disgust and self-hate. We may even take laxatives or make ourselves vomit. The cycle of starvation/bingeing may point to more serious conditions, anorexia and bulimia nervosa, and these need professional help. There can be few people, however, who have been on a diet and not at some time experienced the need to binge. This is the body's natural reaction to too much control – if we resist something we make ourselves want it all the more! By trying to avoid things in our lives, we make them more likely to happen. In the same way, when we resist food, or certain foods, we make ourselves want it – or them – all the more. The more we control ourselves, the more the pressure builds up, until we can't stop ourselves any longer.

Binge-eaters tend to be impatient perfectionists who see life in black and white. They are either dieting or not dieting. When they are 'dieting' they are ultra-strict; when they are 'not dieting' they are uncontrolled. If they lapse when they are dieting by having, say, a cream cake, they are inclined to feel that because of this 'all is lost' and they might as well give up for the day and start again tomorrow. So they clear the fridge, the biscuit tin, anything that's around, whereas if they'd just allowed themselves the cake little 'harm' would have been done.

As the reasons for binge-eating are often more to do with your feelings than your body, looking at this aspect of your life, can be extremely helpful. You might ask yourself, for instance, whether in fact you really need to slim? Many binge-eaters have a grossly exaggerated view of their size. They take out their feelings of dissatisfaction with themselves by imagining that they are much larger than they are. Then they impose over-strict diets on themselves which they can't keep to, and so they binge. The result is that they are filled with self-disgust and their feelings of loathing towards themselves are confirmed. Having a beautiful body starts with loving yourself, being kind to yourself and making life as easy as you can for yourself. For more about this, see Learning to Love Yourself, page 262.

As I explained on page 16, there may be emotional reasons behind your inability to get slim. Sometimes, for instance, slimness is something which we impose on ourselves with our minds when emotionally – or even physically – we feel more comfortable the way we are. We may need the protection which extra weight gives because we feel too vulnerable without it. If this is so, we will lose weight successfully, and keep it off, when we discover and come to terms with the underlying emotional issues. For more about this, see the section on page 255. In addition, if this is a serious problem for you, some counselling or psychotherapy could be helpful.

10 Do you eat because you are bored/stressed/angry/unhappy?

We often turn to eating in order to comfort us when we

35

feel uneasy. If I have a difficult phone call to make or a demanding piece of work to do, for instance, I find that I will put it off – and comfort myself at the same time – by eating something sugary or starchy. Looking to food for comfort – or because we are bored – can easily become a habit and lead to unwanted weight. Once you realise what is happening, however, you do not have to be a victim of this pattern.

The first step is to recognise when you are eating because you are feeling uncomfortable in some way. Think back to times when you have turned to the biscuit tin or to sweet things. What were you feeling at the time? Once you realise what is going on, you are halfway towards a solution. Next time you feel the urge to eat something sugary or starchy, notice how you are feeling. Are you bored? Angry? Hurt? Putting off doing something because you find it stressful? Unhappy? Are you coping with these feelings by eating, instead of expressing them? And how is your body behaving? Where are you feeling the tension? Relax, shrug your shoulders, let go. Move away from the kitchen or the biscuit tin, lie down and take a few minutes to do the curl-up-your-toes relaxation exercise described on page 270. Or do something that you really enjoy, that isn't connected with food or eating, such as having a bath or a shower. (Yes, you *can* spare yourself this time. And, strangely, when you do this, you will actually have more time to give to other people.)

Many of us go through most of our lives out of touch with our feelings. Or we may be in touch with our feelings, but unable to express them to other people. So again, they get bottled up inside us, stored as emotional energy, which can so often also mean stored physical energy, in the form of fat.

There are two parts to this. Firstly, we have to become

aware of what we are really feeling (not what we *think* we are feeling, or what our minds tell us we *ought* to be feeling). And secondly, we need to know how to express our feelings effectively. For more about this, see the section on page 255.

You will now have a much clearer idea of what foods you are eating and the pressures which make you want to eat. This will help you to plan a diet which you can keep to because it fits in with your lifestyle, includes foods you really like, and feels harmonious to you.

GETTING STARTED

The Vegetarian Slimming Plan (see page 77) is simple and can be varied in a number of ways, in order to make the diet your own. Remember to choose foods you really like. Make slimming a joy and create for yourself a new way of eating which you will love, and which will keep you slim and healthy for life.

Check your weight on the day you begin your diet, and write it down, together with the amount of weight you intend to lose. Many slimming books advise you to weigh yourself at the beginning of a diet and then just once a week after that. If you have your own scales, however, I think it is helpful to check your weight every day. If possible, weigh yourself first thing in the morning, without any clothes on, and before you have had anything to eat or drink. Otherwise, choose the same time of day, and wear the same amount of clothing.

It's interesting to record your weight-loss on a graph and most encouraging to see the downward trend as the pounds drop off. To make a graph, find a piece of squared or graph paper and decide the range of weights you want the graph to cover. This might be from a few pounds more than your present weight down to a few pounds less than your desired maximum weight. Mark the left-hand margin with 500 g/1 lb intervals and the bottom margin with dates, allowing one or two squares for each day. Put a dot on the graph for today's date and weight, and continue each day, or each week. (See the example opposite.)

Your weight will certainly fluctuate from day to day, depending on various factors such as the amount of bulk you have in your bowel and, for most women, the time of the month. However the graph will show you the overall trend as well as the day-to-day changes. This is why I think it is helpful to weigh yourself every day. If you only get on the scales once a week, and for some reason you hit an abnormal day, you do not realise this and cannot have such a clear idea of the trend.

If you feel disheartened – which happens to every slimmer from time to time – think how the pounds mount up. If you lose a steady 1 kg/2 lb a week, that's over half a stone in a month: in eight weeks from now you could be over a stone lighter! It is true that some weeks you may lose less than 2 lb, although even half a pound is worthwhile if you think of the size of half a pound of butter!

Most slimmers hit a plateau at least once during their diet, when their weight just seems to stick obstinately and won't move, whatever they do. But it *will*, if you persist. The great thing is not to give up at this point. Just keep on with the diet, be extra kind and gentle with yourself, and suddenly you will find that your weight starts to move again – in fact, you might find that you lose several pounds all at once!

As the pounds drop off, enjoy the experience of being at each particular weight. Notice how your body looks and feels; how it changes. Really *enjoy* the experience. When you are loving and tender towards your body, you will be amazed at how it begins to feel and look good, like a plant which is being nourished and watered. You will feel a sense of inner peace and harmony which will help you to keep to – and truly enjoy – your diet.

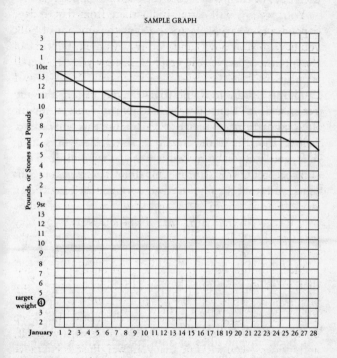

SAMPLE GRAPH

When you set your target, decide how much weight you want to lose, but don't impose a definite time limit. That is setting yourself up for failure, especially if you're unrealistic in your expectations. Simply resolve that this is the amount of weight you want to lose, and that this time you will do it, however long it takes.

TIPS FOR SUCCESS

MAKE UP YOUR MIND TO SUCCEED

Choose an affirmation (a positive statement in the present tense, such as 'I am slim and happy', which you repeat often, as explained on page 281), and use this whenever a 'failure' thought comes into your mind. See yourself in your mind's eye as slim – exactly as you would like to be. Cut out pictures of slim models from magazines, if this helps, and stick them to the fridge door or the biscuit tin!

MAKE A SLIMMING BOOK

It's helpful and fun to make your own slimming book. Stick the graph of your weight at the beginning of the book, then take a page for each day and record what you ate, how you felt, what you did – anything which seems interesting. Write down positive things which people say to you, and any affirmations you may be using. Stick into this book any pictures of slim models which you find inspiring, or fashion and beauty ideas which appeal to you, funny jokes about slimming . . . anything you find helpful.

ENJOY YOUR SLIMMING

Resolve to make this time of slimming a time for *you*. Think of ways in which you can make life as simple and pleasant as possible. Aim to spend as little time in the kitchen as you can. (The Vegetarian Slimming Plan has been designed with this in mind.) Use the extra time to do some of the things you have been wanting to do, but have been too busy to indulge in. This is an ideal time to stock up on those books you've been longing to read, start a new hobby, or begin taking a new and enjoyable form of exercise.

Write two lists in your diet book: one of all the things you enjoy doing, such as going for a walk, reading a book, putting your feet up and listening to music; and the other of all the treats you can give yourself, such as an aromatherapy or revitalising bath (see pages 65 and 70), a new magazine, some flowers . . . write down whatever appeals to you, and add to the list as you think of more things. Make this a really special time when you spoil yourself, and allow your body to become its own slim and beautiful self.

It's a good idea to promise yourself a special reward either when you reach your final goal, or at intermediate goals, say every 3 kg/7 lb, or every 6 kg/1 stone. Make the rewards things which really please you, preferably not food, although you can choose something really indulgent to eat as long as you allow for it in your Calorie count. Another incentive which some people find helpful is to buy themselves a skirt or pair of trousers in the size they plan to reach (or an intermediate size if they have a lot of weight to lose) and then try them on periodically until they fit – or become too loose!

BANISH BOREDOM

If in the past you have eaten through boredom, make a list in your diet book of enjoyable and productive things which you can do instead of eating. This might include some of the treats from the list of things you enjoy, as well as useful jobs which you would like to get done, such as writing letters, tidying out a drawer, sticking photographs into an album, sewing on a button, and so on.

It can also be very helpful to plan your day so that you know roughly what you are going to do at certain times, including watching favourite programmes on television, to prevent that aimless, restless feeling which can lead to over-eating. Do think about the timing of your meals, too. If, for instance, you find it helpful to have your evening meal late, or to save some fruit or a treat from earlier in the day – part of lunch, or breakfast, for instance – to eat later when you know a snack may cheer you up, by all means do so.

JOIN A SLIMMING CLUB OR SLIM WITH A FRIEND

The support and encouragement of other people can be enormously helpful when you're slimming. You can get this, as well as expert advice, by joining a slimming club (consult your Yellow Pages to find one in your area). Or consider slimming with a friend, so that you can spur each other on and have someone to talk to when the going gets tough . . .

MAKE LIFE EASY FOR YOURSELF

When you want to lose weight, it's important to make life as easy for yourself as possible. Aim to make it easier to succeed than to fail by following these tips:

• If you're tempted by snacks, keep away from places where they're sold, or situations where you feel you may be tempted by them. Take care to be out of the room when the snack trolley comes round at work; at home, don't have snack foods in the house. Let other members of the family be responsible for buying and looking after their own snacks if they want them. If they object to this, tell them the reason – that you want to lose weight and when you have these foods it is difficult for you to resist them. Ask for their help and support over this. (See page 258 on Communicating.)

• Instead of cakes, biscuits, crisps and sweets, stock up with fruit and the kind of vegetables that you can nibble, such as cucumber, radishes, carrots and celery. Keep them prepared and ready in the fridge, together with one or two of the low-Calorie dips on page 178, for when you feel you must have something to munch. This may seem quite hard at first, but it is surprising how quickly you lose the taste for sweet things if you persevere. People often find that they begin by nibbling a lot of raw vegetables and fruit to make up for the lack of sugary snacks, but after a few days they lose the need for these, too.

• Plan the quantities for a meal carefully, so that there won't be enough for second helpings.

• Put all the food out on plates. Don't put dishes of food on the table for people to help themselves – otherwise it's too easy to over-eat!

• If you like plenty to eat at mealtimes, fill up with lots of salad or cooked vegetables. Choose ones you really like, from the 'free' list on page 93.

• If you tend to nibble left-overs after the meal, get someone else to clear away the plates (as soon as you have finished eating) and put the remains straight into the bin.

• If you nibble while you're making a meal, plan to do

the preparation at a time when you don't feel like eating (such as after breakfast or lunch), or when you know that your willpower is at its strongest. In any case, while you are dieting, it is a good idea to spend as little time in the kitchen as you can. That is why all the slimming plans given are based on simple meals which require the minimum of preparation, and the recipes in this book are all quick and easy to make. Even if you like cooking, you might consider having more ready-made meals while you're slimming, to make life easier for yourself. It's worth trying some of the low-Calorie ranges. Read the labels to make sure they are suitable for vegetarians, and for food-combiners if you're slimming by that method.

• Eat more slowly. Aim to be the last to finish instead of the first. Take a long, slow breath before you begin to eat and put your knife and fork down between each mouthful. Take sips of water during the meal – even fill yourself up by drinking a glass of water before the meal.

• Make each meal special. Avoid grabbing food and eating it standing up. Think about what you are going to eat; choose foods you really like, and arrange them attractively on a plate. Put flowers on the table or tray, even if it's just for you – perhaps I should say *especially* if it's just for you! Then take the time to sit down to eat your meal, however simple, in a relaxed way, and really allow yourself to enjoy your food. This increases your feeling of well-being and self-worth which, in turn, will help the slimming process. (See page 262 for more about this.)

• Experts often advise us not to eat while we are doing something else, such as watching television or reading a book. This is because it is easy to nibble too much without thinking, if your mind is on something else. So this is something to consider. However, if I'm eating on my own, I have often found it helpful to prepare a meal of my favourite foods and then to allow myself the luxury of eating them whilst putting my feet up listening to music, watching television, reading a book, or even sitting at my word-processor! I think the trick is to plan the meal in advance, so that you have just the right quantity of food, rather than bowls of snack foods such as peanuts, which are easy to keep nibbling while doing something else.

• It's worth asking yourself whether there are certain situations when you tend to over-eat. Then you can plan ways to make such situations easier; or try to avoid them altogether while you are trying to lose weight. (See also Eating Out, pages 106 and 145.)

WHAT EXERCISE DO YOU ENJOY?

One of the funny things about exercise is that the more you do, the more you want to do. The thought of exercise may seem very unappealing at first; you may resist it, and you may feel guilty for not doing it. However, once you make a start, you will feel differently. So, my advice is to start very gently. Don't set your sights too high, and choose a form of exercise which you really enjoy and find easy to do. If you have little time, choose something which easily fits into your lifestyle, such as walking to the station instead of taking the car, cycling to the shops, getting out the skipping rope while the children are watching a programme on television, walking up and down stairs, and so on. Once you start these simple forms of exercise, you will want to do more, and could consider fitting in other things too, such as going swimming, taking a regular brisk walk each day, joining a yoga class, or taking an exercise class, to tone up as you lose weight. But first, get started. Start simply, but start today. Here are some suggestions for practical and effective forms of exercise when you are slimming.

A SIMPLE STRETCHING, BENDING AND TONING ROUTINE

This is a simple routine which only takes a few minutes. It can be practised on its own to make you more flexible, or it can be used as a warm-up routine before other forms of exercise. It makes an ideal preliminary to the slimmer's yoga routine (page 50).

STRETCHING AND BENDING

1   Stand erect with your feet about 45 cm/18 in apart, hands at your sides. Lift your arms up and clasp your hands, palms upwards, above your head. Link your fingers, then stretch up as high as you can, keeping your feet on the ground. Return your hands to your sides, then repeat the stretch twice.

2   Now lift your arms and interlock your fingers as before, but this time bend first to the right, and then to the left. Return to the starting position, then repeat twice.

3   Lift your arms and interlock your fingers as before, then bend forwards from the tops of your legs, keeping your spine straight (see diagram).

4   Then lift up and bend backwards gently as far as you can. Return to the starting position, and repeat twice.

5   Lift your arms but don't interlock your fingers this time; then bend down as if you were trying to touch your toes. Keep the back of your legs straight, but do not strain.

BUST TONING

This isn't really a warm-up exercise, but it is a valuable, quick toning exercise which fits easily into this routine.

Standing or sitting, raise your arms straight out in front of you, then clasp each elbow with the opposite hand. Push with each hand, as if you were trying to push your arms away from each other. There will be no movement, just a feeling of tension in your arms and at the sides of your chest and breasts. Hold for a count of 10, gradually increasing to 20. Repeat twice.

LEG LIMBERING

Lie down on your back with your legs extended and your arms by your sides. Complete this routine first with the right leg, then go right through it again with the left leg.
1   Bend your right knee and pull it up towards your chest. Repeat several times.
2   Lift your right leg up vertically. Put your hands behind your knee and pull it towards your chest, keeping your leg straight. Then lower your leg to the floor.

TUMMY, HIP AND THIGH TRIMMING

Remain lying down, with your legs together and straight out in front of you and your hands by your sides. Now lift your feet and legs about 15 cm/6 in off the ground. At the same time, lift your head and neck. And bend your knees slightly so that your calves are parallel with the floor. You will feel the tension all down your body. Hold the position for as long as you can, then relax. Repeat twice. Gradually increase the length of time that you hold the position.

WALKING

Start by walking briskly for 10–30 minutes, and gradually build up your speed and the distance you cover as you get fitter. You may like to combine walking with a bit of jogging. I find a combination of walking and running works extremely well: 20 paces walking, 20 paces running. Aim to go fast enough to feel glowing, but not so fast that you become breathless. (You should be able to talk as you walk.) Warm up beforehand by doing a few minutes of the gentle bending and stretching exercises described above, and do the same to cool down at the end of your exercising. Make sure you have comfortable running shoes which support your ankles well and have plenty of cushioning in the sole. It is worth going to a sports shop and trying on a number of pairs until you find the ones which feel best.

SKIPPING

Skipping is another excellent form of exercise. Actually you don't even need a skipping rope: you can just jump and make the arm movements as if you had a rope, although it is more fun with a rope. Make sure you have comfortable shoes, and, again, start slowly, with perhaps 30 skips on the first day. Increase the number by 10 a day. Skipping is a demanding form of exercise which burns up the Calories well. Aim eventually to skip for perhaps 10 minutes, but break this up into several shorter sessions of 2 minutes throughout the day.

SWIMMING

Swimming is one of the best forms of exercise because it burns up Calories but does not overstrain the heart, and it can be enjoyed by people who are overweight or who have stiff joints because of the support the water gives.

If possible, choose a time when the swimming pool is least crowded, and start by swimming gently to warm up. Then, using whichever stroke comes most naturally to you, swim 4 lengths (of a 25 m/27 yd pool). Rest for a minute, then repeat, alternating your favourite stroke with lengths of backstroke or sidestroke if you can. Gradually build up the number of lengths you swim, week by week: 8 lengths, as described, the first week, 10 lengths the second week, 12 lengths the third week, and so on. Pause for a moment between lengths if you need to. When you are swimming 20 lengths, you will be swimming 500 metres, which is about a third of a mile, and swimming this distance at least three times a week will certainly help you to lose weight.

As your fitness increases, you will be able to add more lengths. Always start and end with a length or two of gentle swimming to warm up and cool down. You might then like to break up your swimming time into two 15-minute periods, and see how many lengths you can do in each; it is very rewarding to watch your ability gradually increase. But don't push yourself so hard that you don't enjoy the exercise! When you are swimming on your front, aim to get your face down into the water: it is helpful to have a pair of close-fitting goggles to prevent your eyes getting sore.

A SLIMMER'S YOGA ROUTINE

Yoga is excellent for general health and flexibility. It is always a good idea to attend a yoga class if you can, so that a qualified teacher can check that you are doing the poses correctly. It's also helpful to have the moral support of the class. In the meantime, however, here is a simple yoga routine to get you started. All the poses are particularly good for slimming and toning. You'll need a mat, folded blanket or large towel which you keep for practising your yoga (and for doing your relaxation).

Remember never to strain in yoga. Progress comes through regular, gentle practice. Always breathe through your nose; never hold your breath. Usually you exhale as you do a movement which needs particular effort, but if you are not sure about the breathing, just breathe normally. This routine takes about 30 minutes, and consists of the following poses:

- The Mountain
- The Triangle
- The Staff
- The Forward Bend
- The Twine
- The Cobra
- The Locust
- The Bow
- The Shoulder Stand
- The Plough
- Relaxation

THE MOUNTAIN

This is the starting point for a yoga routine. Stand upright, with your feet together and parallel, your heels and big toes touching, arms loosely by your sides. Feel yourself standing as if you are firmly rooted to the ground. Pull up from the arches of your feet; tighten the backs of your knees, stretch up the backs of your thighs, pull your stomach in and stretch your spine up, as if you are being pulled upwards by a piece of string attached to the crown of your head. Keep your shoulders, face, throat and hands relaxed. Make sure you are evenly balanced on your feet, not tilting either forward or back. Rest in this position for a moment or two, then you are ready to begin.

THE TRIANGLE

An excellent general stretching posture, good for loosening your hips and making them more flexible, so that you can do the bending postures more easily, and for toning and slimming the waist, hips and thighs.

1   Stand in the Mountain posture, then 'jump' your feet about 1 m/1 yd apart. Turn your right foot out 90 degrees, and your left foot in slightly. Breathe in and raise your arms to shoulder level.

2   Exhale, and bend to the right, sliding your right hand down towards the floor. Your left arm remains straight and will now be up in the air. Look up towards the left

thumb. Hold, breathing normally, then breathe in while standing up. Repeat with the left side.

Note: Do not allow your hips to turn; keep them facing forwards all the time. One way of ensuring that they face forwards is to do the pose with your back against a wall.

THE STAFF

This improves your posture, strengthens your back, and is the starting point for the next two postures.

1   Sit on the floor with your legs stretched out in front of you and your back straight – you might find it helpful to do this exercise against a wall to ensure that you keep your spine straight. Sit well forward on the bones of your pelvis, with your hands on the floor beside you, fingers pointing towards your feet.

2   Hold the position for as long as you can without strain, then repeat twice more.

THE FORWARD BEND

This is one of the most important yoga postures, benefiting the spine, the heart and the abdomen. You may find it difficult to stretch very far at first, but if you do this bend every day you will progress, little by little, until one day you'll be able to hold your feet with your hands, put your head on your knees, and rest and relax in this position for 5 minutes!

1   Sit in the Staff position as described above. Keep your feet relaxed.

2 Reach forward with your hands and slide them down your legs as far as you can, still holding them comfortably without hunching your back. Different people may be able to reach calves, ankles or feet.

3 Now take a deep breath and as you breathe out pull yourself forward from your hips, attempting to get your ribcage flat on top of your legs and your head down. Breathe normally while you hold this position for a few seconds. Relax, then hold the position again; relax and then repeat.

Note: If you are very stiff, use a belt or a scarf around your feet to help you gently pull yourself down and your chest forward. Even if you are very stiff to start with, you will gradually make progress.

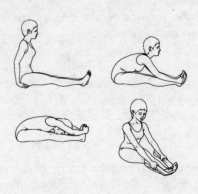

THE TWINE

This is a good exercise for general toning and flexibility and it helps you to lose weight in the waist and hips.

1 Start in the Staff posture as described above, then bend your knees and move both legs round to the right of your body beside your hips. Make sure your knees are

together. Sit up straight, then put the fingers of your right hand under your left knee, with your palm on the floor.

2 Bring your left arm behind your back and try to get hold of your right arm above the elbow. Turn your head to look over your right shoulder.

3 Breathe normally. Hold the pose for 30 seconds, gradually increasing the time, then repeat with the other side.

THE COBRA

This, and the next two poses, form a sequence and are very pleasant to do. The Cobra increases flexibility in the spine, firms the neck and bust and slims the hips, but it is important to bend gently and not to strain at all.

1 Lie down on your front, with your forehead on the mat. Place your hands, fingers forwards, beneath your shoulders.

2 Breathe in and, as you do so, slowly arch your neck and raise your head, pushing on the floor with your hands. Keep your spine curved and your head back.

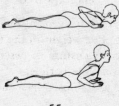

3   Continue to breathe, raising your head and upper body as high as you can.
4   Hold the position for 20 seconds.
5   Gradually come down, reversing all the movements. Relax, then repeat twice more.
Note: Your hips should always be on the floor.

THE LOCUST

The Locust firms hips and thighs.
1   Still lying on your front, rest your chin on the floor. Have your hands pointing forwards beneath your shoulders. Inhale, and raise the right leg as high as you can; hold the position for a count of 10, then slowly return your leg to the starting position. Repeat with the left leg.
2   Now lift both legs together, as high as you can, and hold the pose for 10 seconds.
3   Slowly lower your legs. Relax, then repeat the whole sequence twice more.

THE BOW

The Bow firms bust, waist, hips and thighs. Rest your chin on the mat. Bend your legs at the knees, stretch back with your hands and hold your ankles. Pull on your ankles, and raise your head, chest and thighs, to give a bow-like posture. Hold the final position for 10 seconds, then slowly relax, but continue to hold your ankles. Repeat the pose twice more.

THE SHOULDER STAND

The Shoulder Stand is one of the most powerful postures in yoga, resting the internal organs, relaxing the legs and stimulating the thyroid gland which helps to control weight.

1   Lie on your back on the floor and place your hands beside you, palms down.

2   Swing your legs back so that your hips leave the ground. Place your hands on your hips to support them.

3   Straighten your legs and body, pointing them towards the ceiling. Your chin should be close to your chest.

4   Breathe naturally; hold this position for 20 seconds to start with, gradually increasing the time until you are holding it for 5 minutes.

5   Gently bring your legs down and return to the starting position, or go straight into the Plough, which follows on from the Shoulder Stand.

Note: Do not attempt this posture if you have high blood

pressure, without professional advice. It's best to avoid the Shoulder Stand and the Plough when you have a period.

THE PLOUGH

This has the same beneficial effects as the Shoulder Stand and also relieves stiffness in the back and shoulders.

1   Start by doing the Shoulder Stand as described above. Then slowly lower your legs to the floor, over your head.

2   Keep your legs and back straight – don't sag!

3   When you are steady, stretch your arms back towards your feet. Remain in this position for 20 seconds at first, gradually building up to 5 minutes, as with the Shoulder Stand.

4   Before you come out of the pose, stretch out your arms behind you, to give an extra stretch to your spine, then gently bring your legs back over your head and relax on your mat for a minute or two.

Note: If you cannot get your feet down on to the floor, put a chair or similar object behind you and lower them on to that. Be careful with this pose if you have lower back problems.

RELAXATION

The Plough completes the series of exercises, but it is a good idea to follow with a few minutes of relaxation – perhaps with the relaxation technique described on page 270 – if you have time. Remain lying on your mat, but cover yourself with a rug to make sure you are warm enough.

THE BENEFITS OF EXERCISE

Ideally the gentler forms of exercise – such as yoga – should be practised in addition to another, more energetic type which gets you moving, gets the blood pumping round your body and burns up the Calories. I like the concept of the body as a heat-engine in which we take in fuel in the form of food and combine it with oxygen to release chemical energy. If we take in more fuel than we need, as we know only too well, this is likely to be stored as fat. The more exercise we do the more oxygen is pumped round the body. This means that more fuel is burnt and less is likely to be stored.

If you really want to burn up energy, you should ideally aim for 30 minutes of non-stop, energetic exercise, such as brisk walking or swimming, at least five times a week, to get the oxygen pumping round. This should be combined with a daily workout of stretching and bending exercises, such as yoga postures, to keep you flexible. Another form of exercise which can be enormously helpful is bioenergetics. This is described in *The Way to Vibrant Health* by

Alexander Lowen (page 304). Others might find the practice of T'ai Chi Ch'uan, or other more active martial arts, stimulating and health-promoting. Whatever you do, however, start gently.

Exercise has many benefits. It helps you feel good about yourself, develop a firm, lithe shape, feel more energetic, and more 'alive' and active. You may need less sleep as your energy levels are boosted. And, contrary to what many people believe, you will also find that your craving for food disappears.

HERBS, FOODS, LOTIONS AND POTIONS
Herbs and Foods

Some foods have properties which make them especially helpful when you are slimming, and you might like to experiment with these to help speed up your weight-loss. Generally the foods need to be eaten raw in order to get the maximum benefit – the delicate substances which give them their helpful properties are destroyed or impaired by cooking.

In addition, a diet consisting of a high percentage of raw fruits and vegetables – around 75 per cent – has been found to reduce appetite as well as to speed weight-loss. Such a diet is described in detail on page 149. Of course this only works if you like raw fruit and vegetables; if not, there's no point in trying to make yourself eat them simply in order to try to speed up your diet. Because of their excellent properties, though, you might like to introduce more raw fruits and vegetables gradually, choosing the ones that you like best, and noticing the effect which they have on you and your weight.

VEGETABLES

• **Asparagus, lettuce, cucumber, fennel** and **celery** all have a diuretic effect, helping the body to get rid of fluid, which is particularly beneficial in treating cellulite.

• **Beetroot** eaten raw is said to help the body to break down and eliminate fat deposits; in fact beetroot has been found to be a potent healer generally, and particularly in work with cancer patients.

• **Cabbage** is not specifically helpful for slimming, although the fibre and vitamins which it supplies are valuable. However all members of the cabbage family contain substances called indoles which are thought to be natural cancer-inhibitors.

• **Carrots** eaten raw are naturally cleansing, as well as being rich in protective beta-carotene and vitamin C.

• **Dandelion** is another very useful ingredient, and a traditional herbal remedy for obesity. Both the leaves and the root are valuable. Pick tender leaves from a plant which grows well away from exhaust fumes and other pollutants, wash thoroughly, chop and add to salads. The recommended 'dose' is 6 leaves daily! Alternatively, take dandelion root in the form of coffee, which you can buy from healthfood shops. If you find you do not like the flavour of 'neat' dandelion coffee, it can be mixed with ordinary coffee. (Ordinary coffee is itself a diuretic, and I have to say that at the time of writing I personally drink both coffee and tea rather than the herbal alternatives.)

• **Kelp and other seaweeds** are useful because they are rich in iodine, stimulating the thyroid gland and helping to speed up the metabolic process. If you find seaweeds unpalatable, try taking kelp tablets, which you can buy from healthfood shops.

● **Spinach** not only contains chlorophyll but also oxalic acid, which, when taken *uncooked*, has a cleansing effect on the digestive system and speeds up the elimination of waste products.

● **Sprouted seeds** which you can buy at healthfood shops, or grow yourself at home much more cheaply (see page 157), have many health-giving properties, including certain compounds which help the body to metabolise fats.

There are recipes using many of these ingredients in the recipe section of this book, and some of them can also be made into juices (see page 64).

FRUITS

As with vegetables, there are some fruits which are particularly effective in helping the body to shed excess weight.

● **Apples** are a notable natural healing remedy, containing substances which help to cleanse the system, as well as valuable fibre.

● **Blueberries** are diuretic.

● **Cider vinegar**, made from apples, is one of those ingredients which has had many claims made for it in the past, including the ability to speed weight-loss. For this, cider vinegar is generally taken as a drink, 1 tablespoon in hot water, perhaps sweetened with a dash of honey.

Whether or not cider vinegar can help weight-loss, it does contain malic acid which aids digestion. An excellent way to get the benefits of cider vinegar is to use it in place of other vinegars in salad dressings.

• **Grapes** have been used for years as a natural cleanser in 'the grape cure' when you just eat grapes. A day on grapes can be very restful and cleansing, as well as helpful from the slimming point of view. Eat nothing else but grapes (up to 2.5 kg/5 lb), with spring water to drink.

• **Kiwi fruit, mango, pawpaw** and **persimmons** all contain an enzyme called papain which helps the stomach to digest protein.

• **Pineapple** contains an enzyme called bromelain which helps digestion. I have found a day on raw pineapple (if your teeth can stand it!) particularly valuable in pulling off the pounds at the beginning of a diet. The Pineapple and Banana Emergency Diet (page 115) is also very effective.

• **Strawberries**, like pineapple, contain bromelain. As well as being effective on their own, they are also very helpful when mixed with buttermilk, as described in the quick diet on page 115.

• **Watermelon** is most effective if you eat it with nothing else for a whole day. Have as much as you want: up to 2 whole watermelons (crunch up the seeds with the flesh, they're delicious and nutty, and packed with useful nutrients). Watermelon is also an effective diuretic, as you will certainly discover!

To benefit fully from these fruits, they must be eaten raw, preferably first thing in the morning (or throughout the day if you are having a day on fruit). They are best eaten on their own, with an interval of 3 hours before or after eating anything else.

JUICES

If you find it difficult or unappealing to chew large quantities of raw vegetables, a juicer could be a good investment. The type I find easiest to use extracts the juice and expels the pulp (rather than collecting the pulp in a filter which has to be cleaned out after you have made a certain amount of juice). Or you can buy organic vegetable juices in healthfood shops. **Carrot juice** makes an excellent base; try mixing this with **apple juice** and a little **celery** and **beetroot juice**; or add small quantities of **cabbage**, **parsley** and **cucumber juice**. A squeeze of lemon juice in the mixture helps to preserve the colour, but it's best to drink the juice straight away.

HERBS AND SPICES

In addition to tasting good, many herbs have useful medicinal properties. Some of the best for slimming are **rosemary** and **sage** (which are also said to improve your memory and to have a generally stimulating and revitalising action). They are strong-tasting, but can be chopped over salads and cooked vegetable dishes, or made into teas (see opposite).

Thyme, **mint**, **marjoram**, **garlic**, **cayenne**, **parsley** and **celery seed**, **aniseed**, **caraway seed** and **dill seed** are all helpful for digestion, and the last five also have diuretic properties. **Fennel seed** is particularly valuable because it is mildly diuretic and also seems to have the effect of suppressing the appetite.

Add any of these herbs to salads, soups, vegetable and main-course dishes.

TEAS

Herb teas can be used to change your mood, ease digestion, and help your body to rid itself of excess fluid.

• **Camomile, lime blossom** or **linden** and **passion
flower tea** relieve tension and have a calming effect.

• **Fennel tea** is one of the most helpful; make this by
putting 1–2 teaspoons fennel seeds into a pot and covering with boiling water in the usual way. Flavour with a
little honey or lemon if you like. Try drinking this tea
three times a day and see what effect it has.

AROMATHERAPY

Aromatherapy is the art of healing using essential oils.
Essential oils are highly concentrated extracts from aro-
matic plants. These essential oils are readily absorbed
through the skin, and the aroma alone can have a subtle
but powerful effect on the mind and body. The body is
able to detect and react to very small quantities of some
chemicals: one drop of the oil galbanum, even when
diluted in an Olympic-size swimming pool, can still be
smelt!

Some of the essential oils used in aromatherapy have
recently been tested in some experiments conducted at
Toho University School of Medicine in Tokyo, in which
volunteers' brain waves were measured. The results corre-
lated well with the responses expected by aromatherapists. For instance, jasmine, which aromatherapists use
for its stimulating, uplifting effect (amongst other properties), was shown to increase the brain waves, whilst
lavender, which is considered to be soothing and balanc-
ing, had the opposite effect.

Aromatherapists use essential oils from plants to treat
many conditions, and to bring balance, health and har-

mony to the whole person. You do not have to be ill, however, to benefit from aromatherapy; the essential oils can be used to ease the stresses and tensions of normal life and can be particularly valuable when you are slimming.

An excellent way to experience the benefits of aromatherapy is to have a professional treatment, which is both healing and a luxurious indulgence that I would recommend to any slimmer. Not only are there essential oils which can help you to continue with your diet and to lose excess fluid, but the very fact of having an aromatherapy treatment helps you to feel good about yourself and about your body. If you have a treatment, your aromatherapist will advise you as to the essential oils which you can use at home, in the bath, or in the other ways suggested below. Or you can select one or two oils which appeal to you, try them out for yourself and see how they affect you.

Because of the body's extreme sensitivity to them, the essential oils need to be carefully distilled and prepared to avoid impurities that could have adverse effects. So be sure to buy the best-quality oils from a reputable supplier, preferably one of the mail-order suppliers mentioned on page 305, or Tisserand or Neals Yard Essential Oils if you want to buy them over the counter. Synthetic oils may smell the same, and have a similar chemical structure, but they do not necessarily have the same effect. True essential oils are expensive, and the more expensive they are, the purer and better they are likely to be. They should be kept in dark glass bottles, tightly stoppered, away from light. Never buy anything purporting to be an essential oil if it is in a clear glass or plastic bottle. Expect to pay varying prices for the different essential oils; the price reflects the rarity of the oil – some are easier to extract than others. The name of the plant should be on the bottle, and the essential oil should not have been diluted nor have had anything added to it or taken away from it.

The oils can be used in various ways. An aromatherapist normally combines them with a 'carrier' oil (a pure vegetable oil, usually grapeseed or sweet almond, perhaps with some wheatgerm oil added, for its natural preservative qualities) to make a massage oil. The quantities are 3 drops of essential oil added to 5 ml of carrier oil, and the oil should be used as soon as it has been made up. You can use the oils in this way at home, particularly in the spinal area, where they are absorbed especially well, or to massage your hips and thighs if you have cellulite, or your feet and legs if they are aching after exercise. Or you can add the oils to a bath, which is what I generally do, using 6 drops to a normal-size bath. You can just add the drops to the bath, or mix them first in a little oil (as above) or in a couple of tablespoonfuls of milk or cream. Take the bath immediately you have put in the oils, as the effect begins to wear off quickly. Never, incidentally, take essential oils internally.

Another way to use the oils is to mix them with water to spray the room. You can use a plastic house plant spray for this: put in 200 ml/7 fl oz water and 20 drops of oil, shake vigorously then spray the room immediately. You can dissolve the oils in 2 teaspoonfuls of vodka before adding them to the water if you prefer. Do not leave the mixture in a plastic spray bottle because plastic and metal (except for stainless steel) interact with the essential oils. A ceramic or glass spray bottle is best. Another excellent way of vaporising the oils is to heat them. You can buy special burners for the purpose; these consist of a nightlight with a dish-like compartment on top to hold water and the essential oil. Again, choose pottery or ceramic material, not metal, and make sure there is a nice big dish section so that you don't have to top it up with water too often. Fill the dish section of the burner with water and add about 12 drops of essential oils. Alternatively, you could simply put a few drops of the oil on to a cotton handkerchief and sniff it.

Each essential oil can be used on its own or you can use several mixed together. For instance, you could try a mixture of **geranium** or **bergamot** oil with **rosemary** or **juniper** as a massage oil for your hips and thighs to help shift cellulite. These oils will also give you a 'lift', help to clear your mind and, in the case of **rosemary**, stimulate you. (Don't use this late at night, when you want to sleep!) **Bergamot** is a particularly useful oil for eating disorders (compulsive eating or anorexia nervosa), because it seems to have the effect of regulating the appetite and bringing balance and harmony to eating habits.

For a relaxing, sleep-inducing massage, **lavender** and **camomile** are both very calming and soothing. A bath with oil of lavender in it, together with **rosemary** or **marjoram**, will help to make you more supple before exercising.

Any of the following oils also help to relieve tension and stress: **bergamot**, which is cheering and uplifting (but should never be used on the skin undiluted or before exposure to strong sun or sunbeds because it accelerates burning); **lavender**, which helps to balance fluctuating moods; **camomile**, which is very soothing; **neroli**, which calms fears (and is excellent for shocks but is very expensive to buy); **clary sage**, which is very relaxing, almost euphoric, but should not be used after you have had any alcohol as it can result in nightmares and unpleasant hallucinations; **frankincense**, which calms emotions linked with the past. If you are feeling very emotionally or mentally drained, **juniper** is a good oil to use, perhaps combined with **bergamot**. **Jasmine** is a most valuable essential oil if you are feeling depressed, lethargic and lacking in self-worth, whilst **rose** is perhaps the greatest treat of all, wonderful when you are grieving, sad or unsure of yourself. Rose can also help a woman to feel more attractive and confident in her sexuality. Don't use rose if you're pregnant, as it has a toning effect on the reproductive organs. Other oils which should be avoided during pregnancy include **juniper**, **basil**, **clary sage**, and **rosemary**. And these last two are also best avoided if you have high blood pressure.

Rose and jasmine are the most expensive essential oils to buy, but superb to use and highly concentrated, so you only need a drop or two in a bath. A tiny bottle of one of these oils would be a beautiful present to give a special friend who is slimming – or to give yourself!

Don't continue using one essential oil repeatedly for more than about two weeks; you could try different oils, or alternate oils which have a similar effect, such as **camomile** and **lavender**. It is important, too, not to use too much of the oils. Rather than increasing the potency, using excessive amounts can actually deaden it, or even produce the opposite effect. Never use an oil if you don't like the smell of it.

If you are using the oils in a bath for children, the quantities need to be reduced (1 drop in a baby bath, 2–3 drops in a normal bath used by a toddler, and up to 4 drops for an older child). Some oils, such as **fennel**, are not suitable for young children. To soothe a child, **camomile** is good, as it is one of the gentlest of the oils, and **lavender**, **rose** and **mandarin** are particularly helpful for children. Always mix essential oils first in oil or milk before adding them to a child's bath.

REVITALISING BATHS

A bath can be both relaxing and revitalising. There are two baths which are particularly beneficial and which you might like to try. These are the *Wechsel-Bad* or alternating bath, and the sitz bath.

For the **alternating bath**, you run a bath in the usual way, making it comfortably hot. Add 1 tablespoon grapeseed oil if you like, and some selected aromatherapy oils if you wish. (These can be added to the grapeseed oil before you put it into the bath.) Wash and relax in the bath. Then, when you feel ready, let out half the water, and at the same time turn the cold tap on full. Lie back, and with your hands mix the cold water in with the warm. Keep mixing as the water gets cooler and cooler. In about 3 minutes, your skin will feel glowing. And, surprisingly, you won't feel cold. Get out of the bath and wrap yourself in a towel, as large and luxurious as possible. Wrap up well and dry yourself. Then, if there's time, lie down in bed for 5–10 minutes, relax and let go of your worries and burdens. You will emerge feeling like a new person!

The **sitz bath** has a similarly invigorating effect, but is quicker. For this, fill the bath with cool (not cold) water, then sit sideways in the bath, with your legs and feet hanging over the side. Remain there for a few minutes, then get out and dry yourself. This bath stimulates the important glands and organs of elimination in the lower part of the body; it has been called the 'youth bath' because of the way in which it increases the circulation and helps to keep you young! Take a sitz bath once or twice a week or whenever you feel like it.

SKIN-BRUSHING

The body gets rid of some waste products through the skin, and by brushing your skin you can help speed up the elimination of toxins. In addition, brushing the skin stimulates your circulation and improves the action of your lymphatic system. Daily skin-brushing will help to tone you up as well as getting rid of cellulite on your hips, bottom and thighs.

All you need is a bath brush with good hard bristles. Make sure these are natural and not nylon. The brush may have a handle or a strap to slip your hand under – it doesn't matter which. Each day before you bath or shower, brush your skin. Start by brushing from your fingertips to your shoulders. Use a firm but comfortable pressure. You may find that the brushing hurts a bit at first, but you will soon get used to it and find it a pleasant sensation. When you have brushed both arms several times, move on to your body, brushing always towards the heart; from the tops of your legs to your chest, up your front, back and sides. Repeat several times, then brush upwards from your toes to your body, brushing each leg 10 times. If you have cellulite around your thighs, hips and bottom, pay particular attention to these areas.

BACH FLOWER REMEDIES

The Bach Flower Remedies are essences, distilled from flowers, each one corresponding to a mental and/or emotional state. Healing comes about through choosing a remedy, or several remedies, based on the patient's personality and mental and emotional state, rather than on their physical symptoms. This system of healing was discovered by Dr Edward Bach in the early part of this century, and is one which I have found to be very helpful.

71

It is great to be able to select a remedy and quickly nip any problem in the bud before the mind and emotions work their way through to the physical body. Bad moods disappear with great speed.

You can easily make up your remedies by buying a stock bottle of a remedy (or the complete set of 38 remedies) and adding 2 drops to some pure spring water in a 30 ml dropper bottle. You then take 4 drops of this mixture in water three or four times a day, or more. Every half hour is very effective.

Bacn remedies are particularly helpful in combating the bad moods, stress and fear that one gets when slimming. For instance, you could try a dose of **centuary** when you are feeling weak-willed or others are encouraging you to give up your diet; or some **beech** if you find yourself being overly critical of your progress (or of other people). **Larch** is a good remedy to take if you lack confidence in your ability to succeed; **pine** if you demand perfection of yourself and have low self-esteem, and it can also help you when you break your diet and feel guilty.

If you get depressed about your progress and feel like giving up – perhaps if you reach a discouraging plateau – **gentian** is the remedy to take; and **impatiens** if you are feeling impatient and tense. **Olive** is good for exhaustion, **rock water** if you are being too strict with yourself, and **crab apple** if you have feelings of self-disgust, feel fat and hate your body. If you swing from one mood to another, or from over-eating to starvation, **scleranthus** is the remedy to take, whilst **chestnut bud** will give you insight into past eating habits, so that you can form new, healthier eating patterns. This remedy is also good if you find that you keep repeating the same mistakes, and lose weight only to gain it all back again quickly.

Walnut will help you to break old eating habits,

willow will melt away resentment and bitterness if you are hanging on to these, along with the weight, and **wild rose** will give you new vitality and enthusiasm for your diet if you've lost your motivation and become resigned to being overweight. If you are feeling really hopeless about your ability to diet, because you've had so many unsuccessful attempts or because you have so much weight to lose, try **gorse**.

Cherry plum is a helpful remedy to take if you lack self-control and find you tend to binge and cheat on the diet, whilst **agrimony** is useful if you need help coping with the emotions that lie behind the eating. If you find that thoughts of food are always on your mind, **white chestnut** will help you, whilst **hornbeam** will increase your willpower and give you the additional strength you need to lose weight. Hornbeam can also relieve the tiredness associated with boredom that leads many of us to over-eat.

You can take several remedies together (simply add two drops from each to your bottle) but it's best not to take more than six at a time. Taking too many tends to cloud the issue so that they do not work so well. Try to decide which are your strongest feelings, and use the remedies for these. When you have finished your bottle, you can always change the remedies. If you are in doubt as to which remedy to take, it can be helpful to write down how you are feeling, as if you were writing a letter to a friend or a consultant. This can enable you to look at the situation objectively. If you really can't decide, or would rather just have one bottle of remedy, buy a bottle of **rescue remedy**, which is a blend of five remedies, and the nearest thing to magic that I know. I always carry a bottle of rescue remedy in my bag; it is amazingly effective in cases of shock, emergency or nerves. It could certainly help you through the difficult patches of slimming.

For more about Bach Flower Remedies and how to prescribe them, see the booklist on page 304.

COLOUR

Our choice of colour – in our clothes and our homes – not only says something about how we feel about ourselves and our lives, but can also affect our mood and feelings. **Black**, for instance, shows a desire to blot out, to negate, and it is interesting how many overweight people choose to dress in this colour. Usually this is because, at a mental level, they think that it will make them look slimmer. But what does this colour say about their feelings about themselves? Black is a colour connected with sorrow and grief; it puts things on hold. Wearing it may mean that a woman has a subconscious desire to remain fat to protect herself from her own sexuality. She is afraid of being a woman, so she wears black to keep herself safe and secure. Black will hold you in position, prevent you from straying from the subject in hand. It can be an aid to concentration and a path to freedom, but when you are overweight, it can keep you stuck that way.

Dark grey can show sabotage and self-deception, also criticism and depression, although a **pale, silvery grey** is uplifting. It calms the emotions, brings illumination, spiritual harmony and peace of mind, especially when combined with **rose pink**, both colours being used in moderation. **Pale pink** on its own – the colour of a ballerina's shoes – shows a young girl's dream and, in the case of older women, a desire to hark back to the past. Perhaps her present life needs looking at, to see ways in which this can be made more fulfilling.

Pale pink is also a great solvent; it melts away and helps

74

to disperse old, rigid patterns and thoughts. It is a good colour for relieving depression. The positive aspects of this colour are unselfishness to the point of sacrifice, for the benefit of the whole, physical perfection, and warmth to relieve harshness. However an excess of pale pink can lead to weakness, misunderstanding and grave errors of judgement. A **deeper rose pink** is a colour of love, comfort and forgiveness. It helps where there is conflict and struggle, but too much of this colour can be overbearing and focus things too much on the physical senses.

Blue is a soothing, healing colour. It brings harmony – perhaps at any price. It is a colour that preserves the status quo, keeps things as they are, so it is not a good colour to wear or to have around you if you want to lose weight. **Red** is a strong, powerful, invigorating colour, great when you need energy and vitality, and a good detoxifier, helping you to get rid of rubbish from your body and your life. But it can be tiring if overdone. **Yellow**, too, is a detoxifying colour; it is also joyful and stimulating, and will brighten and activate your mental processes: I have known of people who have had insomnia when sleeping in bedrooms decorated in this colour. A change of colour scheme – to pink – led to an instant cure!

Green is a harmonising colour and gets rid of negative emotions and mental stress. It helps you to get to the root of the problem, to make up your mind and to make clear decisions. Green can help you to become more assertive; it is a gateway to freedom.

Orange has the effect of breaking up old conditions to prepare for the new. It's a sociable colour and gets you moving physically, so it's particularly good for slimmers. It's stimulating and warming and helps you to piece your life together again after traumatic experiences, grief or divorce.

Red, orange and yellow are particularly good colours to wear when you're wanting to lose weight. You do not have to dress from head to toe in these colours for them to work for you; a blouse, scarf or sweater is enough, or, if you loathe the colours, consider wearing them as underwear!

Incidentally, there is a theory that weight drops off more easily if you wear natural fibres such as cotton and wool, which are 'in tune' with the body, instead of synthetics. I have found this to be true in my own case.

Part 2
The Vegetarian Slimming Plan For Calorie-Counters

This is an effective slimming diet based on fresh fruits and vegetables, grains and pulses, with optional small quantities of dairy produce. The Vegetarian Slimming Plan is effective because:

- It's simple – just choose your meals
- It's easy – little cooking is needed
- It puts you in control – you can include your favourite foods
- It works – because it is based on the tried-and-tested Calorie system.
- And it can be adapted to suit different lifestyles

MAKING IT WORK FOR YOU

The Vegetarian Slimming Plan is based on 1000 Calories a day, but more foods can be added from the Diet Boosters (see page 93) if you need to slim on a higher number of Calories. If you are a woman with less than 6.5 kg/1 stone to lose, 1000 Calories should give a pleasing weight-loss of around 1 kg/2 lb each week. However, if you have more than 6.5 kg/1 stone to lose, you could start at 1200

Calories, and if you have over 19 kg/3 stone to lose, you could start at 1500 Calories. It is best to start with these higher allowances, and then reduce your Calorie intake as you lose weight. You will still lose weight fast, and may in fact lose more than 1 kg/2 lb a week to start with, because the more you weigh, the more quickly the weight comes off. When you get to within 6.5 kg/1 stone of your ideal weight, you can reduce your daily Calorie allowance to 1000 which will help to pull off the final pounds quickly.

If you are a man, you will lose weight quickly on 1200 Calories. But if you have more than 6.5 kg/1 stone to lose, you should boost the diet to 1500 Calories to start with.

HOW THE DIET WORKS

Each day, you may have: *CALORIES*
- 300 ml/10 fl oz (½ pint) skimmed or soya
milk, or 150 ml/5 fl oz full-fat milk   100
- 2 pieces of fruit (apple, orange, pear or
banana), to eat whenever you like, after meals, or
as snacks   100
- Breakfast   200
- Lunch   250
- Evening meal   350
- As many vegetables as you want from the 'free' list on page 93
- In addition, if you are slimming on 1200–1500 Calories a day you can have extra items chosen from the Diet Boosters on page 93, or the Treats on page 94, to a value of 200–500 Calories
- Black tea and coffee without sugar, and slimline drinks, as you wish

VARYING THE DIET

Although, for convenience, this diet is planned in the form of meals, these can be varied in many ways. For instance, you can:

● **Make swaps**

Swap your day's fruit allowance (or milk allowance, if you like your drinks black) for food from the Diet Boosters (page 93) or Treats (page 94) lists, or any other item, to the value of 100 Calories. Or you could swap your breakfast, lunch or evening meal for foods of 200 Calories, 250 Calories or 350 Calories respectively. Alternatively, you may want to have a lunch or breakfast menu instead of an evening meal one. This would save you 100 or 150 Calories that you could then use for another food.

● **Have a bigger evening meal**

You may choose to save Calories by having a lighter breakfast and lunch and then adding extra items to your evening meal. Eat your day's fruit allowance for breakfast, saving 200 Calories, and allow yourself 2 pieces of fruit from the Fruit List (page 94), or 1 piece of fruit and 1 very low-fat yogurt for lunch, saving 150 Calories, 350 Calories in all. You can then, in effect, have a double evening meal, adding extra items from the Diet Boosters (page 93), including a pudding from this book (pages 231–242), or a favourite bought pudding.

● **Eat the meals as snacks**

As many of the meals are made up of several simple foods, you can easily divide them up and eat the items at different times. Some slimmers like to put all their food for the day together, like a big picnic, and then dip into it as and when they want to. One advantage of this method is that once you have got the food together, you can forget about it until you eat it, and you can spend the absolute minimum amount of time in the kitchen.

THE MEALS

Suggestions are given here for breakfast, lunch and evening meals. For the evening meal there are two types: extra-quick ones which require the minimum of cooking, and meals made from recipes in this book. These are quick, too, but obviously need a bit more preparation. You can also use vegetarian convenience meals to the value of 200–250 Calories, plus salad from the Free Vegetables (page 93), for lunch. And for the evening meal, vegetarian convenience meals to the value of 300–350 Calories, plus salad or cooked vegetables from the list of Free Vegetables.

As previously mentioned, the code ⓥ indicates that the meal is suitable for vegans as suggested or in one of the variations.

QUICK BREAKFASTS

(200 Calories)

YOGURT, FRUIT AND TOAST

150 ml/5 fl oz plain low-fat yogurt with either 1 teaspoon honey or 75 g/3 oz chopped fruit; 1 piece of wholewheat toast with scraping of butter, margarine or low-fat spread

CEREAL AND TOAST ⓥ

20 g/¾ oz unprocessed breakfast cereal (such as bran flakes or 2 wheat breakfast biscuits) with skimmed milk or soya milk, no sugar; 1 piece of wholewheat toast with scraping of butter, margarine or low-fat spread

FRUITY MUESLI Ⓥ

Muesli made with 15 g/½ oz oats, 15 g/½ oz
wheatgerm, 15 g/½ oz sultanas, 1 grated apple,
moistened with a little skimmed milk, soya milk or
orange juice

CEREAL AND FRUIT Ⓥ

25 g/1 oz unprocessed breakfast cereal (such as
bran flakes or 2 wheat breakfast biscuits) with
skimmed milk or soya milk, no sugar; 1 piece of
fruit, such as an apple, pear, orange or half a large
banana

COMPLETE MUESLI

Mix together 15 g/½ oz oats, 15 g/½ oz wheatgerm,
100 g/4 oz plain low-fat yogurt, 1 grated apple

GRAPEFRUIT, ROLL AND HONEY Ⓥ

½ grapefruit, 1 crusty roll, 2 teaspoons honey or
low-sugar preserve

JUICE AND CEREAL Ⓥ

150 ml/5 fl oz orange juice, 25 g/1 oz bran flakes,
150 ml/5 fl oz skimmed milk or soya milk

SCRAMBLED EGG ON TOAST

1 egg scrambled with 2 tablespoons skimmed milk
and 1 piece of wholewheat toast

TOAST AND HONEY OR MARMALADE ⓥ

2 pieces of wholewheat toast with either a scraping
of butter, margarine or low-fat spread or 2
teaspoons low-sugar marmalade or preserve

YOGURT AND HONEY

150 ml/5 fl oz plain low-fat yogurt, with 1 teaspoon
honey and large chopped banana

PORRIDGE

Stir 25 g/1 oz rolled oats and 150 ml/5 fl oz water
in a pan over a medium heat for 2 minutes until
thickened. Serve with either 1 teaspoon honey or
brown sugar, and either 150 ml/5 fl oz skimmed
milk or 2 tablespoons single cream

EASY LUNCHES

(250 Calories)

BAKED POTATO LUNCH ⓥ

175 g/6 oz baked potato with 25 g/1 oz cottage
cheese or 1 tablespoon soured cream mixed with
chopped chives, or 25 g/1 oz sweetcorn or cooked
beans, and as much salad as you want

CRISPBREADS, CHEESE AND SALAD

4 Ryvitas, 40 g/1½ oz Edam cheese, as much salad
as you want

JUMBO SALAD SANDWICH ⓥ

Jumbo salad sandwich made from 2 slices of
unbuttered wholewheat bread and as much salad
as you want

RYVITA, CRISPS, CHEESE AND SALAD

25 g/1 oz packet potato crisps, 1 brown Ryvita
topped with 25 g/1 oz thinly sliced Edam cheese
and as much salad as you want

BEANY SALAD ⓥ

Half a 400 g/14 oz can beans or chickpeas, drained
and mixed with chopped onion, any chopped fresh
herbs available, 2 teaspoons olive oil and 1
teaspoon vinegar, served with salad

COTTAGE CHEESE, RYVITA AND SALAD

100 g/4 oz cottage cheese served with raw
vegetables such as strips of red pepper, carrot,
spring onion, celery, cucumber, with 2 Ryvitas
spread with scraping of butter, margarine or low-
fat spread

MUSHROOMS ON TOAST WITH SALAD ⓥ

225 g/8 oz mushrooms fried in 1 teaspoon butter,
margarine or olive oil and served on 2 slices of
unbuttered wholemeal toast, with as much salad as
you want

GREEK SALAD AND RYVITA

Greek salad: 100 g/4 oz Feta cheese, diced and mixed with sliced tomato, onion, cucumber and 3 sliced black olives, served with 1 Ryvita

ROLL, CHEESE AND SALAD

1 crusty roll, 25 g/1 oz Edam cheese, as much salad as you want

FILLED PITTA POCKET Ⓥ

1 large wholemeal pitta pocket packed with chopped salad: lettuce, tomato, cucumber, onion, grated carrot and any other Free Vegetables (page 93), plus either 25 g/1 oz sliced Edam cheese or 75 g/3 oz drained cooked or canned beans, chickpeas or sweetcorn, if liked

TOMATO AND CHEESE ON TOAST WITH SALAD

1 sliced beefsteak tomato on 1 piece of unbuttered wholemeal toast, topped with 40 g/1½ oz thinly sliced Edam cheese and 2 tablespoons grated Parmesan, with as much salad as you want

YOGURT, FRUIT AND A CRUNCHY BAR

150 ml/5 fl oz plain low-fat yogurt, with either 1 chopped apple, orange or pear, or 1 teaspoon honey, and 1 Jordan's crunchy bar

EVENING MEALS

(350 Calories each)
EXTRA-QUICK AND EASY EVENING MEALS

BAKED BEANS ON TOAST WITH SALAD Ⓥ

175 g/6 oz baked beans on unbuttered wholemeal
toast, as much salad as you want

AVOCADO SALAD Ⓥ

Half an avocado with lemon juice and a large salad

CHEESE AND PICKLE ON TOAST WITH SALAD

1 large slice wholemeal toast, 2 teaspoons pickle or
chutney, 40 g/1½ oz Stilton cheese, as much salad
as you want

PIZZA SALAD

150 g/5 oz wholemeal pizza slice, as much salad as
you want

MAIN-MEAL BAKED POTATO Ⓥ

275 g/10 oz baked potato with 1 of the following:
50 g/2 oz cottage cheese; sweetcorn or cooked
beans; 15 g/½ oz grated Edam cheese; 1 teaspoon
butter or margarine; or 1 rounded tablespoon
soured cream and chopped chives. Serve with as
much salad as you want

OMELETTE, RYVITAS AND SALAD

An omelette made with 2 eggs and 2 teaspoons
butter and a filling of tomato, herbs, mushrooms
or asparagus; 2 Ryvitas; salad or steamed Free
Vegetables (page 93)

RICE WITH STIR-FRIED VEGETABLES OR SALAD Ⓥ

50 g/2 oz (dry weight) rice, boiled and served with
350 g/12 oz vegetables stir-fried in 2 teaspoons oil;
or flavour the cooked rice with chopped fresh
herbs, or use pilau rice from a packet but measure
quantities carefully; serve with a large salad
dressed with 2 teaspoons olive oil and wine vinegar
or lemon juice

PASTA AND SALAD Ⓥ

50 g/2 oz (dry weight) pasta, cooked and served
with 1 teaspoon butter, margarine or olive oil and
1 tablespoon grated Parmesan cheese, served with
tomato or other type of salad. (Vegans should
increase the weight of pasta to 65 g/2½ oz and
leave out the Parmesan.)

VEGETARIAN CONVENIENCE MEAL WITH VEGETABLES Ⓥ

Any vegetarian convenience meal up to 300
Calories, served with as many Free Vegetables
(page 93) as you want, steamed or made into salad

QUICK HOMEMADE PIZZA WITH SALAD ⓥ

Spread 1 round pitta pocket with 1 tablespoon
tomato purée, top with slices of tomato and onion
and 25 g/1 oz sliced Edam cheese. Or, for vegans,
spread pitta with 2 teaspoons olive oil, add tomato
purée, tomato and onion, and top with black olives
(chopped, if you like). Bake or grill until pitta
bread is heated through and cheese melted and
golden brown. Serve with as much salad as you
want from Free Vegetables list (page 93).

FRENCH BREAD AND CHEESE WITH SALAD

50 g/2 oz French bread with 25 g/1 oz mature
Cheddar cheese and a salad of lettuce, tomatoes,
cucumber, celery and spring onions

EVENING MEALS BASED ON RECIPES IN THIS BOOK

GREEK SPINACH PIE, TOMATO, LETTUCE AND ONION SALAD

A portion of Greek Spinach Pie (page 216), served
with a salad made from sliced tomato, shredded
lettuce and chopped onion

VEGETABLE GOULASH WITH SOURED CREAM AND FRENCH BREAD

Vegetable Goulash with soured cream (page 198),
served with 25 g/1 oz slice of French bread, and a
green salad (no dressing) if you like

PROVENÇAL STEW AND A BAKED POTATO ⓥ

Provençal Stew (page 194), with a 100 g/4 oz baked potato, and an optional salad made from 'free' vegetables – perhaps watercress and sliced radishes (no dressing)

CHEESE FRITTERS, GREEN BEANS AND TOMATO SALAD

Cheese Fritters (page 219), with a slice of lemon, and steamed green beans, and a salad of sliced tomatoes

SPAGHETTI WITH TOMATO SAUCE AND GREEN SALAD ⓥ

Spaghetti with Tomato Sauce (page 225), served with a salad made from 'free' green vegetables, perhaps including sliced green pepper and cucumber and a few onion rings

FRENCH ONION QUICHE, SALAD OR GREEN BEANS OR COURGETTES

A slice of French Onion Quiche (page 214), served with a large salad made from 'free' vegetables, perhaps including grated carrot, sliced tomatoes, lettuce, chopped herbs, or steamed green beans, or very lightly steamed courgettes

MUSHROOM RISOTTO, STEAMED BROCCOLI OR A LARGE SALAD ⓥ

Mushroom Risotto (page 228), served with steamed broccoli or a large salad made from 'free' vegetables (no dressing), perhaps sliced fennel, red pepper and watercress

FETTUCINE WITH RED PEPPER AND SALAD ⓥ

Fettucine with Red Pepper (page 222), with a salad made from continental leaves, or any other leafy salad greens available

HAZELNUT ROAST, APPLE SAUCE OR MANGO CHUTNEY AND A LARGE SALAD OR COOKED VEGETABLES ⓥ

A slice of Hazelnut Roast (page 211), served with 2 tablespoons apple sauce or 1 tablespoon mango chutney and cooked vegetables of your choice, such as cauliflower and spinach, or a large salad including some chopped celery, dressed with lemon juice

BUTTERBEANS BAKED WITH A HERBY TOPPING, LETTUCE, TOMATO AND ONION SALAD ⓥ

A portion of Butterbeans Baked with a Herby Topping (page 206), served with a salad of shredded lettuce, sliced tomato and onion, and a squeeze of lemon juice

RATATOUILLE, BAKED POTATO, OR PASTA OR RICE ⓥ

Ratatouille (page 197), with a 225 g/8 oz baked potato or 50 g/2 oz (dried weight) pasta or rice

SPICY BEANBURGER IN A BUN, WITH SALAD ⓥ

A Spicy Beanburger (page 208), served in a burger bun, with some lettuce, tomatoes, cucumber and spring onions (or other salad as available, from 'free' list)

TAGLIATELLE WITH CREAM AND BROCCOLI, AND TOMATO SALAD

Tagliatelle with Cream and Broccoli (page 224), served with a salad made from sliced tomatoes, a squeeze of lemon juice and some chopped fresh herbs (basil, chives or parsley) if available

EASY CHILLI WITH BAKED POTATO ⓥ

Easy Chilli (page 210), served with a 100 g/4 oz baked potato and a salad made from 'free' vegetables, if you like, perhaps including some beansprouts

LENTIL DAL WITH SPICED VEGETABLES ⓥ

Lentil Dal (page 206), served with Spiced Vegetables (page 189)

SLIMMERS' CHIPS WITH BAKED BEANS ⓥ

A half-quantity of Slimmers' Chips (page 201),
served with 300 g/10 oz baked beans and some
salad, if you like

MACARONI 'CHEESE' WITH COOKED
VEGETABLES OR SALAD

Macaroni 'Cheese' (page 227), served with a cooked
vegetable, such as spring cabbage, spinach or any
vegetable from the 'free' list, or a salad, dressed
with lemon juice

MUSHROOMS IN CREAM ON BROWN RICE
WITH STEAMED COURGETTES OR A SALAD

Mushrooms in Cream on Brown Rice (page 230),
served with steamed courgettes or a salad made
from vegetables on the 'free' list, perhaps sliced
lettuce hearts

LENTIL BAKE WITH APPLE SAUCE OR
MANGO CHUTNEY, AND STEAMED
CARROTS AND BROCCOLI OR A LARGE
SALAD ⓥ

Lentil Bake (page 205), with 2 tablespoons apple
sauce or 1 tablespoon mango chutney; steamed
carrots and broccoli or a large salad made from
vegetables on the 'free' list, perhaps including
grated carrot, chopped celery, cabbage and
tomatoes

STIR-FRY WITH MARINATED TOFU ⓥ

A portion of Vegetable Stir-Fry with Marinated Tofu (page 191)

PARSLEY POTATO CAKES WITH SALAD ⓥ

Two Parsley Potato Cakes (page 204), served with a salad of lettuce, grated carrot, sliced red or green pepper and chopped celery or spring onion

AUBERGINE BAKE, BAKED POTATO AND SALAD

A portion of Aubergine Bake (page 195), with a 100 g/4 oz baked potato, and a salad made from vegetables from the 'free' list, perhaps chicory spears and watercress

CHILLI LENTIL LOAF WITH YOGURT AND HERBS, AND A LARGE SALAD OR COOKED VEGETABLES

A slice of Chilli Lentil Loaf (page 209), with 2 tablespoons yogurt and herbs and a large salad without dressing made with vegetables from the 'free' list, perhaps coarsely grated carrot, chopped celery and chopped herbs, or cooked vegetables from the 'free' list

FREE VEGETABLES

You can have as many of these vegetables as you wish:
artichokes, asparagus, aubergines, beansprouts,
broccoli, brussels sprouts, cabbage, carrots,
cauliflower, celeriac, celery, chicory,
Chinese leaves, courgettes, cucumber, French beans,
leeks, lettuce, mangetout, marrow, mushrooms,
onions, parsnips, peppers, radishes, runner beans,
spinach, swede, tomato, turnip and watercress.
Lemon juice and vinegar are also free, and rice vinegar or
balsamic vinegar make wonderful Calorie-free dressings
for salad.

DIET BOOSTERS

	CALORIES
1 apple, orange or pear	50
1 large banana	100
1 piece of wholemeal bread or toast with scraping of butter, margarine or low-fat spread	100
25 g/1 oz (dry weight) rice or pasta	100
100 g/4 oz baked potato	100
1 glass dry white wine	100
300 ml/10 fl oz (½ pint) cider, beer or lager	100
any dessert, bought or from this book, to the value of	200
150 g/5 oz baked beans	100
25 g/1 oz Cheshire cheese	100
100 g/4 oz frozen peas or sweetcorn	100
100 g/4 oz bought oven chips or 200 g/7 oz Slimmers' Chips (page 201)	200
150 ml/5 fl oz carton low-fat fruit or plain yogurt	100
75 g/3 oz cottage cheese	100

FRUIT LIST

Choose your daily fruit allowance from this list, or use these fruits as another way to boost your diet if you are slimming on more than 1000 Calories. Each item is 50 Calories.

1 medium apple, orange or pear
1 small or ½ large banana
75 g/3 oz grapes
100 g/4 oz cherries
2 medium tangerines or satsumas
225 g/8 oz fresh apricots
225 g/8 oz strawberries
225 g/8 oz raspberries
1 large peach
1 large nectarine
½ medium mango
½ medium pawpaw
275 g/10 oz melon (any type), weighed with skin
2 kiwi fruit
3 plums
2 tablespoons sultanas
2 tablespoons raisins
5 dried apricots
3 dried peaches
5 dried or 4 fresh dates
2 dried figs
1 large grapefruit
100 g/4 oz fresh pineapple

TREATS

	CALORIES
1 small packet of crisps	150
50 g/2 oz salted or dry-roasted peanuts or cashews	300

50 g/2 oz chocolate, milk or plain	300
50 g/2 oz rich fruit cake	300
2 choc chip cookies	100
1 small Danish pastry	200
1 jam doughnut	200
1 medium currant scone or bun with 7 g/¼ oz butter	200
1 standard-size Mars bar	300
1 chocolate eclair with fresh cream	300
50 g/2 oz vanilla, strawberry or raspberry ripple ice-cream	100
65 g/2½ oz croissant and 2 teaspoons jam	300
1 choc ice	200
75 g/3 oz sorbet	100
300 ml/10 fl oz (½ pint) lager, beer or cider	100
1 × 150 ml/5 fl oz glass of wine	100

ADAPTING THE DIET

IF YOU'RE COOKING FOR A FAMILY . . .

Keeping to a diet can be quite challenging when you have to cook for a family too. Breakfast and lunch do not usually present too many problems, but making an evening meal can be a real test of endurance! You may find it helpful to prepare this earlier in the day, if possible, so that you do not have to be in the kitchen later when you may be tired, with many demands being made upon you, and your willpower possibly at a low ebb!

Many of the meals given in the Vegetarian Slimming Plan can be adapted for a family; for instance, baked beans on toast with salad, baked potato with different toppings, Stilton cheese on toast and the pasta and rice meals. The wholemeal pizza slice and quick homemade pizza are also likely to be popular, and can be served with extra baked potatoes for hungrier members of the family; the omelette, too, could be made into a more substantial meal by serving it with good wholemeal bread, as well as salad. Make life easy for yourself by using vegetarian convenience meals whenever possible. The Vegetarian Slimming Plan allows you to have a convenience meal of up to 300 Calories, and this can also be made more substantial by serving it with extra rice, baked potatoes or bread for the rest of the family. Don't try making puddings for the family while you are trying to slim: let them finish the meal with ice-cream, fresh fruit or yogurt.

Many of the recipes in this book will probably be popular with the family. Again, they can be made more substantial with extra rice, pasta, potatoes, frozen peas or sweetcorn, or good wholemeal bread.

IF YOU'RE A VEGAN . . .

The Vegetarian Slimming Plan includes a number of suggestions which are vegan as given, or in one of the variations described. Many of the recipes are also vegan. Vegetarian dishes can often be adapted for vegans by using soya milk instead of cow's milk, tofu instead of cheese, a vegan margarine (or olive oil) instead of butter. Cream can often be omitted altogether without spoiling the recipe, and eggs and cheese sometimes can. In addition, strict vegans may prefer to use sugar instead of honey.

IF YOU'RE COOKING FOR ONE . . .

If you're a single slimmer, I think you'll find the Vegetarian Slimming Plan ideal, because it is based on single
servings of foods which take the minimum amount of
time to prepare. For those who go out to work, many of
the lunch ideas are easy to take with you, which may be
more satisfactory than trying to buy the equivalent at
work. Bought sandwiches and baked potatoes tend to be
high in butter content which can push up the Calories
alarmingly.

If you are eating out in a restaurant at lunchtime, it
might be best to count this as your main 350-Calorie
meal, instead of the evening meal. You could then have
one of the suggested lunchtime meals in the evening. It is
extremely difficult to keep within the 350-Calorie limit
when eating out; saving your fruit and/or milk allowance,
or part of your breakfast, and putting these towards lunch
would give you more flexibility. Or you could consider
this as your main meal of the day, and eat very lightly at
breakfast and in the evening, as suggested on page 79.
Even so, you need to be careful about your Calorie intake;
see tips given under Eating Out (page 106).

IF YOU'RE AN OLDER PERSON . . .

Although many people put on weight as they get older,
this is neither 'natural' nor healthy. An older body is
healthier when it has less weight to carry around, because
this puts less strain on the heart. Although our metabolism slows up a little as we get older, it is still possible to
lose weight steadily and safely on a healthy slimming diet.
And you can improve your metabolism, as well as your
general health, by taking some form of regular exercise, as
described on pages 45–60.

The meal suggestions in the Vegetarian Slimming Plan are all quick and easy to make, and can be prepared in single-serving amounts, or doubled up, for two people. You can have the main meal at midday instead of in the evening if you prefer, and any of the recipes in the Main Meals section of this book (up to 300 Calories) can be used too, for variety. The Quick Vegetable Hotpot (page 200), Nut Burger-For-One (page 212), and the Cheesy Oat and Tomato Bake (page 218) are especially recommended.

For the other meal, soup can make a welcome change. Both the Lentil Soup (page 174) and the Root Vegetable Soup (page 172) are easy to make and low in Calories. A good portion of either of these, and a warm wholemeal roll or good piece of wholemeal bread, with a scraping of butter, margarine or low-fat spread, will come to around 250 Calories, and makes another lunch possibility. These soups freeze well, too.

It's important to make sure you are getting enough vitamins, especially vitamins A and C to fight infection, the B vitamins for the nervous system and general health, and vitamin D for healthy bones. A multivitamin tablet containing these vitamins might be a good idea, particularly if you find it difficult to chew salads. Or you could consider buying a juicer and taking your vitamins in the form of fruit and vegetable juices. Make sure you are getting enough fibre by eating wholemeal bread and wholegrain cereals each day.

IF YOU'RE PREGNANT . . .

It is not advisable to slim during pregnancy unless you are advised to do so by your doctor. It is perfectly healthy, however, to eat a normal, unrestricted vegetarian diet. I have covered this subject fully in my *Mother and Baby Book* (page 303).

IF YOU'RE COOKING FOR CHILDREN . . .

It's miserable for children when they're overweight. It's not a good idea to put them on a strict slimming diet, although there are a number of things you can do to help the situation. Just changing to a vegetarian diet in itself can be enough to enable some children to slim down. Aim to help them hold their weight steady, rather than to lose weight, then the situation will naturally sort itself out as they grow. A vegetarian diet can certainly meet the needs of growing children. If it is a good varied diet with plenty of fresh fruit, vegetables and wholegrains, extra vitamins are not necessary, apart from a vitamin D supplement. For those whose diet is rather low in dairy produce a vitamin B12 supplement is also recommended. If you are giving your child soya milk, buy one which is fortified with extra vitamins: your local healthfood shop will advise you on this.

Children often gain weight in the first place as a result of eating too many snacks and junk foods; when these are cut out, the fat goes too. Simply restricting the junk foods rather than banning them completely – perhaps making them 'for weekends only' – may do the trick. In addition, it is helpful to watch, and reduce, the child's intake of high-fat foods at mealtimes. Cut down on fat in general, and buy low-fat alternatives where possible. Encourage the child to fill up with healthy foods which are naturally low in fat: wholemeal bread; vegetables such as raw carrots, celery and cucumber (whatever they like and will eat!); baked potatoes; pasta; pitta breads filled with chopped salad and drained canned red kidney beans; fresh and dried fruit. Try them with the recipes in this book – especially the ones for cheese and pasta – which are generally particularly popular with children.

Sometimes squash or other drinks tend to aggravate a

weight problem. Not only are these extremely high in sugar, but they can also take the edge off the child's appetite, so that they never eat enough nourishing food at mealtimes, and then fill up with more drinks and snacks later. When the drinks are rationed, with water or sparkling water instead of squashes and cordials, again, they lose weight naturally.

Of course, like an adult, a child may gain weight for emotional reasons. If you have a child with a weight problem, in addition to following the practical suggestions above, it might be helpful to re-read pages 35–37, with your child in mind. First of all, it is important to realise that there is absolutely *no blame* attached to the situation. Do not feel that you have failed in some way if you think your child's weight problem may be due to emotional issues. Emotional issues are part of life: they happen and, life being what it is, there are no such things as perfect parents. It's an impossibility! So relax, try to put your own feelings on one side and consider the situation from the child's point of view.

For instance, the child may feel unable to talk about his or her feelings – and bottled-up emotion can show in the body as fat. In the same way, a child who feels threatened or vulnerable may put on weight – until they feel secure and happy. It is extremely helpful for a child – as for anyone else – to talk about their feelings and their fears. In order to do this, they need to feel emotionally 'safe'. That is, they need to know that the person listening to them loves and respects them for *themselves* and not for what they do; that whether they are 'good' or not makes no difference to this love. They need to know that the person will listen without interrupting; that they will accept what they hear and not react in a defensive, emotional, critical or hurt way.

This means that the person listening needs to be aware of their own feelings as the child talks, but to realise that these have nothing to do with the child, and to put them on one side whilst giving the child full attention. This can be extremely uncomfortable, if what the child is saying is touching raw nerves in the listener. It is painful to feel a child's fear and sadness, especially if there is nothing you can do about it. That is why, if the child is feeling unhappy, the natural reaction is to try to calm them down – 'there, there, don't cry' or 'pull yourself together' or 'big boys don't cry' – but bottling up emotion does not help the child. Being encouraged to feel it, and being allowed to express it, without condemnation, does. You may not be able to take the problem away, but letting a child express their feelings about it is actually the most positive thing you can do. Get into the habit of asking how he or she *feels* about a situation, so that the child realises that they count. Also, if you feel that the child is overweight because he or she is having difficulty with assertiveness, show them ways to get their views across, as described on pages 258–261.

Children – and adults – often comfort-eat because they dislike themselves and do not feel that they are lovable. As they get fatter, they dislike themselves even more, so they eat more, and the vicious circle continues. So help children to feel good about themselves by frequently expressing your love for them. Praise them often for their good points; don't nag them for their bad habits, this only accentuates them. Try praising them for the characteristics you would *like* them to have. Help them to make the most of themselves, to dress in a way which draws out their good points, or which *they* feel makes the most of them (which may not be the same thing!).

CALORIE-COUNTING MADE EASY

This section includes quick guides to Calories in basic foods and toppings. A more complete Calorie-Counter and food-combining table is on page 282.

CALORIE-COUNTING TIPS

As I hope you will have discovered, counting the number of Calories you eat is really not that difficult. Although you need to measure foods to start with, you do get used to the size of portions. An easy way to measure out some foods, such as cooked rice, beans, pasta and vegetables, is to use a 150 g/5 oz cottage cheese or cream carton. Once you have weighed out how much this holds and worked out the Calories, you don't have to be constantly weighing foods. Do be careful about quantities for some foods, though. Whilst an extra few grams of vegetables at around 5 Calories per 25 g/1 oz is neither here nor there, when it comes to cheese, at perhaps 120 Calories for 25 g/1 oz, or nuts at around 170, or butter at 225 Calories, habitually over-estimating could easily slow up your weight-loss.

When you know the Calorie values of foods, you put yourself in control. You can include your favourite foods in the Vegetarian Slimming Plan, and make the diet your own. You will probably be surprised at how quickly you get to know the Calorie values of the foods you eat regularly. Start with a few basic foods (see the table opposite) and build on those. Look up in the Calorie-Counter (page 282), or in one of the many good Calorie books available, the Calorie values of other foods you like to eat. You might like to jot these down in a notebook. Many packets and cans also have the Calorie content of foods on them, written in both kjoules and kcals.

CALORIES IN BASIC FOODS

CALORIES

milk, skimmed or soya (300 ml/½ pint, approx.)	100
cereals, including oats, flour and breakfast cereals (25 g/1 oz)	100
bread, per slice	80
(per 25 g/1 oz)	65
potato, per medium serving (225 g/8 oz)	200
(per 25 g/1 oz)	25
butter and all fats and oils per tablespoon	120
(per teaspoon)	40
sugar (25 g/1 oz)	112
apple, orange or pear (average size)	50
avocado pear (half)	230
cottage cheese (25 g/1 oz)	30
yogurt, plain low-fat (150 ml/5 fl oz)	80
Cheddar cheese (25 g/1 oz)	120
nuts and seeds, on average (25 g/1 oz)	160
pulses, uncooked (25 g/1 oz)	80
pulses, cooked and/or canned (100 g/4 oz)	130
egg (1 whole)	80

Most vegetables are around 5 Calories per 25 g/1 oz and can be considered free items (see page 93), with the exception of the starchy vegetables: potatoes, sweetcorn, peas and beans; and avocado, which is high in Calories because it is oily.

CALORIES BY THE SPOONFUL

Here's a table which shows how many Calories you're adding when you spoon on those sweet or piquant toppings, sauces or extra garnishes. Spoon measurements are, as always, level.

	CALORIES
almonds, ground (1 tablespoon)	40
bran (1 tablespoon)	10
cheese, Parmesan (1 tablespoon)	30
coconut, desiccated (1 teaspoon)	10
cornflour (1 teaspoon)	10
cream, single (1 tablespoon)	30
cream, soured (1 tablespoon)	10
curry powder (1 teaspoon)	12
flour, wholemeal (1 tablespoon)	30
French dressing (1 tablespoon)	75
French dressing, oil-free (1 tablespoon)	6
honey (1 teaspoon)	20
horseradish sauce (1 tablespoon)	13
jam (1 teaspoon)	15
mango chutney (1 tablespoon)	40
marmalade (1 teaspoon)	15
mayonnaise (1 tablespoon)	120
mint sauce (1 tablespoon)	5
molasses (1 tablespoon)	45
mustard, made (1 teaspoon)	10
oil (1 teaspoon)	40
peanut butter (1 tablespoon)	93
pickle (1 tablespoon)	35
piccalilli (1 tablespoon)	15
raisins (1 tablespoon)	30
salad cream (1 tablespoon)	50
salad cream, low-calorie (1 tablespoon)	22

sesame cream or tahini (1 teaspoon)	30
sesame seeds (1 tablespoon)	130
soy sauce (1 tablespoon)	13
sunflower seeds (1 tablespoon)	130
sugar (1 teaspoon)	20
sultanas (1 tablespoon)	30
tomato ketchup (1 tablespoon)	15
tomato purée (1 tablespoon)	10
wheatgerm (1 tablespoon)	30
yeast extract (1 teaspoon)	9

FAST FOODS, TAKEAWAYS AND CONVENIENCE FOODS

Fast foods which are suitable for vegetarians include pizza with a vegetable and cheese topping, vegetable curries and birianis, baked potatoes, Chinese vegetables and rice, chips, and sandwiches without meat or fish in the fillings. Pizzas are high in Calories, between 700 and 900 Calories, although if you're sharing a pizza, a 150 g/5 oz wedge comes to just 300 Calories.

Curries and birianis are high in Calories and probably best avoided while you're slimming: a vegetable curry with rice comes to around 1000 Calories. Chinese takeaways are better, but stick to plain boiled rice. Baked potatoes are good: basic Spud-U-Like potato is 240, or 325 with butter. With baked beans but no butter these potatoes are 320; 340 with sweetcorn, 510 with cheese and onion, 465 with coleslaw, and 480 with soured cream.

Chips, at around 350 Calories for a small serving, are higher in Calories than plain baked potatoes, for about half as much potato, but if you eat them as a main course with salad – which is the way I think chips should be eaten – they can make a useful fast-food meal.

Sandwiches vary, depending on the filling. Plain salad sandwiches (without mayonnaise) are lowest, at around 250 Calories for two; egg and salad sandwiches are about 300; while cheese sandwiches tend to be rather high in Calories, perhaps around 400 Calories for two.

EATING OUT

Eating out is so much easier now for vegetarians than it was even a few years ago. Many pubs and restaurants have at least one vegetarian dish on their menu, and the number is increasing as the demand grows. Unfortunately, however, many of the dishes which are most frequently offered – such as lasagne, quiche, ploughman's lunch and stuffed pancakes – are not particularly helpful to the vegetarian slimmer because they are very high in Calories. So eating out requires some care, particularly if you often eat in restaurants. Nevertheless it *is* possible, especially if you can look upon it as an interesting challenge to see how few Calories you can 'spend'. Keeping your slimming goal in mind, and enjoying the company and the ambiance, will take your mind off the food.

When eating out, you can 'save' Calories by remembering the following tips:
• Refuse optional extras, such as bread rolls before the meal and chocolate mints afterwards.
• If you want to drink, keep to one small (142 ml) glass of wine, which is less than 100 Calories, but ask for mineral

water as well. This will quench your thirst, while helping to drink the wine slowly and make it last.

• Start to eat last, taking a deep breath and relaxing before you do so.

• Put your knife and fork down between each mouthful, as this will also help you to eat less.

If you follow these guidelines, and choose carefully from the menu, there is no need for a meal out to spell disaster for your diet. Starting with the first course, melon, grapefruit or tomato juice are the best bets, at less than 50 Calories each. A plainly cooked vegetable such as asparagus, artichoke or corn on the cob is also a good choice, but ask for it to be served with lemon juice and no butter or dressing. Clear soup, too, is low in Calories, but make sure that it hasn't been made with meat or fish stock. If none of the starters offered seem low enough in Calories, it is sometimes possible to ask for a small salad without dressing, or some crudités, or a small plate of steamed vegetables without butter, instead. So do ask, and explain why. (Being assertive and getting your needs met in this way will help the slimming process, too, as explained on pages 255–262.)

When it comes to choosing a main course, one of the best options is simply to ask for a plate of cooked vegetables without butter – ask for some fresh lemon wedges to squeeze over them – and grind over some black pepper, too. In a way, I'm sorry to suggest this option after all the efforts we vegetarians have made to get something more adventurous on to menus. But because vegetarian main dishes are made up of a number of ingredients, often including some high-Calorie items such as oil, cheese and nuts, it's not as easy to pick a low-Calorie dish as it is for meat-eaters, who can order something like plainly cooked chicken, lean meat or fish and know where they are, Calorie-wise.

Bean-based dishes, which you might get at a vegetarian restaurant – or baked beans, at a canteen – are usually modest in Calories, as is pasta if it's served plain (without oil, butter or creamy sauces) or with a simple tomato sauce. Spaghetti Napolitana is always a good dish to order, along with a side salad without dressing. If the portions of pasta are too generous, feel free to leave some, and keep within your Calorie allowance! Pizzas, on the other hand, are not a good choice, because, as mentioned above, they are between 700–950 Calories each, depending on their depth and toppings.

The food at Indian and Middle Eastern restaurants tends to be very oily, and therefore high in Calories, although a vegetable curry with plain rice is a possibility, particularly if you eat sparingly and leave some. Chinese vegetarian dishes can be good if you stick to plain boiled rice and stir-fried vegetables. Surprising though it may seem, chips, at around 350 Calories a portion, can make a good choice if eaten as a main course, with plain cooked vegetables or salad (no butter, sauces or dressings). As a general rule, however, avoid foods which have been fried, or which contain cheese, oil or nuts, as well as those cooked with creamy sauces.

When it comes to the sweet course, there are fewer low-Calorie options. Fresh fruit salad or strawberries, without cream, are possibilities, at around 50 Calories, or a small portion of sorbet. A cup of black coffee is probably the best ending, though.

ENTERTAINING

Entertaining is a particular challenge when you're on a diet, but it need not mean that slimming has to be abandoned! It is helpful to do the cooking at a time when you have plenty of energy and your willpower is high: early in the day, or after you have eaten a good meal. The following menus are made up from recipes in this book and they each come to between 320 and 580 Calories per serving. This is higher than the main-meal allowance of 350 Calories in the Vegetarian Slimming Plan, so if you are entertaining it might be best to save some Calories from your other two meals that day. Or you could save your fruit allowance for a couple of days before you entertain, to allow you some extra Calories. In these suggested menus the extras, shown in brackets, can be offered to your guests but are not included in the Calorie total.

LIGHT LUNCHES

(v) *Approximately 320 Calories*
Chilled Root Vegetable Soup (page 172)
(Warm poppyseed rolls)
Fresh Asparagus and Mushrooms in Filo Baskets (page 213)
Lightly cooked baby sweetcorn, courgettes and mangetout
Lettuce salad with purple onion rings
Lemon Sorbet (page 236)

Approximately 420–520 Calories
Asparagus with lemon juice and black pepper
Spinach Roulade (page 220)
(New potatoes with chopped parsley)

Lightly cooked baby carrots
Tomato salad with chopped fresh basil
Peaches in Wine (page 239)

WITH A GREEK FLAVOUR

Approximately 420–520 Calories
Tsatsiki (page 181) on lettuce hearts (with warm pitta
strips)
Greek Spinach Pie (page 216)
Aniseed Carrots (page 186)
Tomato, Cucumber, Onion and Black Olive Salad
Greek Fruit Salad (page 242)

Approximately 540 Calories
Hummus (page 182) with raw vegetables (and warm pitta
strips)
Ratatouille (page 197)
Rice with chopped fresh herbs
Green beans
Lettuce heart salad
Grape and Peach Fruit Salad (page 242)

WITH AN ITALIAN FLAVOUR

(V) *Approximately 560 Calories*
Artichokes with lemon juice and black pepper
Tagliatelle with Spring Vegetables (page 224)
Fennel, Red Pepper and Carrot Salad (page 160) with
black olives
Blackberry Sorbet (page 235)

Approximately 490 Calories
Herbs and Flowers Salad (page 163)
Mushroom Risotto (page 228)

Watercress and Tomato Salad (page 161)
Pears in Wine (page 239)

WITH A FRENCH FLAVOUR

Approximately 490 Calories
Marinated Melon (page 183)
French Onion Quiche (page 214)
(New potatoes)
Tomato Salad with chopped fresh basil
Courgettes
Quick Yogurt Pudding (page 238)

Ⓥ *Approximately 580 Calories*
Mushroom Pâté (page 181)
Provençal Stew (page 194), made without mushrooms
(Baked Potatoes)
Green salad
Tofu Fruit Fool (page 233)

FEEDING A CROWD

Approximately 360 Calories
Pimento Lasagne (page 226)
Green salad
Orange Cheesecake (page 236)

Approximately 660 Calories
Jacket potatoes with a large variety of different toppings,
for people to help themselves
Coleslaw (page 159)
Tomato and onion salad
Fennel, Red Pepper and Carrot Salad (page 160)
Orange Cheesecake (page 236) or Chocolate Ice-Cream
(page 231)

CAN YOU DRINK AND DIET?

Alcoholic drinks are high in Calories, so if you drink more than the occasional glass of wine or half-pint of beer or lager, you soon use up your Calorie allowance and run the risk either of having a very unbalanced diet, or of failing to lose weight. Also, alcohol has the effect of relaxing your willpower and giving you a craving for more sugar. However, bearing these disadvantages in mind, if you enjoy a drink, and can limit the amount, there is no reason why you shouldn't allow some Calories for alcohol. If you want to include a drink in your day's menu, save Calories as suggested, and swap them for a drink. It's a good idea always to order mineral water as well as an alcoholic drink, and drink them alternately. Not only is this the best way I know of avoiding a hangover, but it really does help to make the alcoholic drink last a lot longer! If you are drinking spirits, it's best to dilute them with plenty of mixer, making sure it's a slimline one. In general, the drier the drink, the fewer Calories it contains.

BOOZE GUIDE

	CALORIES
300 ml/10 fl oz (½ pint) beer or lager	100
300 ml/10 fl oz (½ pint) cider (all types except vintage)	100
glass of sherry, 57 ml/2 fl oz	70–80
glass of wine, 142 ml/5 fl oz	100
spirits, per pub measure	55
vermouth, per pub measure	53–90

THREE QUICK DIETS

THE RICE AND FRUIT DIET

I gave this quick diet in my book, *The Green Age Diet* (page 303), but I am repeating it briefly here because it is simple and effective, and very useful if you want to get your diet off to a good start, to give your metabolism a boost when you hit a plateau, or to get rid of the last few obstinate pounds. The original rice diet was developed by Dr Kempner at his clinic in County Durham, USA, and is fully described by Judy Moscovitz in her book *The Rice Diet Report* (page 304). This version is based on an allowance of around 600 Calories a day. It's strict and some people find it quite monotonous, so you probably won't want to stay on it for more than a day or two, or perhaps 14 days at most. (Having said that, some severely obese patients of Dr Kempner remain on rice and fruit for many months.) It is possible to lose a considerable amount of weight in a short time on this diet: ½–1 kg/1–2 lb a day during the first week is not unusual.

The Rice and Fruit Diet consists of:
- Three meals a day, each based on fruit or fruit and rice
- Tea, herb tea or decaffeinated coffee, without milk, sugar or sweeteners
- No soft drinks of any kind
- No salt, pepper or other flavourings except for freshly squeezed lemon juice
- Homemade lemonade, made with freshly squeezed lemon juice and low-Calorie sweetener

BREAKFAST

1 piece of fruit

LUNCH

2 pieces of fruit
100 g/4 oz cooked rice (white, brown or Basmati), no
salt

EVENING MEAL

2 pieces of fruit
100 g/4 oz cooked rice (white, brown or Basmati), no
salt

A 'piece of fruit', as far as this diet is concerned, is an apple, banana, pear, mango, wedge of melon, or the equivalent in smaller fruits, such as 4 fresh apricots or 2 peaches or 225 g/8 oz soft fruits such as strawberries, raspberries or cherries.

Choose fruits you really like, and add variety by having different types of rice (except wild rice, which isn't a true grain), so that losing weight becomes a really joyful experience. You may be surprised at how good such simple food tastes.

The combination of rice and fruit seems to result in the best weight-loss, but a possible variation is to have a tomato salad instead of one of the fruits. Make this by slicing and mixing together 2 large tomatoes, ¼–½ an onion and ¼–½ a green pepper. Dress with a little lemon juice.

You can also have 1 glass of dry white wine instead of a piece of fruit as an occasional treat!

TWO ONE-DAY EMERGENCY DIETS

Here are two crash diets, which you follow for 1 day only, to get back on the rails after you have eaten too much, or to lose ½–1 kg/1–2 lb quickly.

PINEAPPLE AND BANANAS

In my experience, this is an amazing diet which can get rid of 2–2¼ kg/4–5 lb. You have fresh pineapple for breakfast, lunch and your evening meal. Then, last thing at night, at least 2 hours after your last meal of pineapple, have 2 large bananas. Nothing else is allowed except water, black coffee, tea or herb tea without milk. No sugar, lemon, sweeteners or slimline drinks.

STRAWBERRIES AND BUTTERMILK

Another combination which is excellent for getting rid of ½–1 kg/1–2 lb overnight. You just have 3 × 300 ml/10 fl oz cartons of buttermilk and 1 kg/2 lb strawberries. They can be blended together into a milkshake or the strawberries can be frozen and then whizzed with the buttermilk to make a thick ice-cream. Nothing else is allowed except water, black coffee, tea or herb tea without milk. No sugar, lemon, sweeteners or slimline drinks.

COMING OFF THE DIET AND STAYING SLIM

Once you have reached your goal weight, you need to find the number of Calories that you can eat each day to keep your weight steady. The best way to do this is to increase your allowance by 200 Calories a day for a week, then weigh yourself. If you haven't gained weight, next week add on another 200 Calories each day. Continue like this until you find the Calorie level at which you gain weight, then go back to the previous level.

People develop different ways for keeping their weight steady. Some continue to watch what they eat during the week but indulge themselves more at weekends; others eat normally most of the time, but may have one day a week when they eat very lightly, perhaps just eating fruit.

It's a good idea to continue to weigh yourself regularly. You will probably find that your weight fluctuates a bit. The important thing is not to let it get out of hand. Now you have lost weight, you know you can do it! So make up your mind never to get more than 3 kg/7 lb above your goal weight, and if your weight creeps up, either go back on the Vegetarian Slimming Plan, or have a few days on the Rice and Fruit Diet, or a day on one of the quick diets, followed by a few days on the Vegetarian Slimming Plan. That should do the trick! If you feel yourself slipping back into old ways, re-read the sections in the book on eating habits, and also on using affirmations. It may be helpful to look at what is going on in your life and consider the reason *why* you are eating more, and perhaps make some changes. Be kind to yourself; maybe you're going through a time when you need more nurturing and love.

Your awareness of yourself and of your eating habits, together with your knowledge of food values, and increased physical exercise will enable you to remain slim, healthy and full of vitality.

The Vegetarian Slimming Plan For Food-Combiners

This is an alternative style of slimming if you prefer not to count Calories. There are a number of diets which are based on food-combining, including the Hay System, the Beverly Hills Diet, and Fit for Life, each with slight variations. The basic principle of food-combining is the same, however. Since proteins need an acid environment for digestion, and carbohydrates need an alkaline one, the body can digest them more easily and efficiently when they are eaten separately. Excess weight is shed; there is a feeling of inner harmony and the body is able to heal itself. This theory is controversial and has been scoffed at by some scientists and nutritionists. However those who try it usually find that it works; not only do they lose weight, but they also feel better and, in particular, digestive problems are eased or cured. I personally find that I feel good when I eat compatibly and I like to eat this way most of the time.

MAKING IT WORK FOR YOU

Proponents of compatible-eating diets maintain that you lose weight because the body is able to deal more efficiently with food. I have found that you can certainly lose weight on this type of diet; you do not need to count Calories, but you still need to eat fairly simply. So I suspect that at least part of the slimming effect may be due to the natural limitation of choice which eating compatibly entails! I recommend this form of dieting wholeheartedly, with one proviso: if you over-eat, whether on proteins or carbohydrates, you will still put on weight, whatever combination you eat them in! But if you follow the diet as outlined here, you will find it a very convenient and pleasant way of slimming without having to count Calories. And you may experience other health benefits, too, such as easing of any digestive problems, arthritis or skin problems.

As I mentioned above, apart from the basic rule of not eating proteins and carbohydrates at the same meal, each food-combining diet has slight variations. My version is closest to the Hay System, which I have found the easiest to follow in practice. Dr Hay's philosophy was that food should be delicious so that a diet is easy to keep up, and the Hay System certainly is.

HOW THE DIET WORKS

- Proteins and carbohydrates are eaten separately, never at the same meal.
- Proteins and carbohydrates can be combined with any vegetables (*except* potatoes with proteins) and any fruits which go with them (see table opposite).
- Leave 3 hours between meals, to allow food to be digested.
- Fats mix well with vegetables and carbohydrates but need to be used sparingly with proteins.

• At least one meal a day should consist only of raw fruits and/or any vegetables *except* potatoes.
• Don't use sugar or artificial sweeteners or products containing these, such as slimline drinks. A little honey or real brown sugar can be used with carbohydrate meals.
• Use butter rather than margarine.

FOOD GROUPS

DON'T MIX

CARBOHYDRATES	PROTEINS
Bread	Milk
Cereals	Yogurt
Flour	Soft cheeses
Oats	Hard cheeses
Rice and other grains	Whole eggs
Pasta	Tofu
Potatoes	Wheatgerm
Chestnuts	Pulses
Pulses	Nuts and seeds (not
Lager	peanuts)
Beer	Dry wine
	Dry cider

FRUITS	FRUITS
Ripe bananas	Apples
Dates, fresh and dried	Apricots, fresh and dried
Figs, fresh and dried	Blackberries
Grapes, extra sweet	Blueberries
Pawpaw, if very ripe	Cherries
Pears, if very sweet and	Currants – red, black,
ripe	white
Currants, dried	Gooseberries, if sweet and
Raisins	ripe

Sultanas

Grapefruit
Grapes
Kiwi fruit
Lemons
Limes
Loganberries
Mangoes
Melons
Nectarines
Oranges
Pawpaws
Pears
Pineapples
Prunes (for occasional use)
Raspberries
Satsumas
Strawberries
Tangerines

MIX WITH EVERYTHING

VEGETABLES
All, except for potatoes
Herbs and spices
Grated orange and lemon
rind
Tomatoes

FATS
Butter
Margarine
Soured cream
Egg yolk
Mayonnaise made with
egg yolk
Oils
Olives
Avocado

ALCOHOLIC DRINKS
Whisky

Points to note:

- Margarine is not recommended.
- Melon is best eaten alone, as a fruit meal.
- Pulses are half protein, half carbohydrate and are generally treated as proteins. It's best not to mix them with other proteins, carbohydrates, or fruits, just with vegetables.
- Nuts and seeds are technically neutral. They mix with carbohydrates, but it's helpful to consider them as proteins when planning vegetarian meals.
- Raw tomatoes can be used freely, but cooked tomatoes should be limited to not more than two servings a week. It's best not to have them with carbohydrates because of their acidity.

THE MEALS

- Keep meals as simple as possible while you are losing weight. The simpler your meals, the better this diet will work for you.
- As a general rule, start the day with fruit. If this does not appeal to you, have porridge, or toast and butter or, for a treat, a croissant. It's best to have an all-vegetable lunch – a large salad dressed with lemon juice and a little oil, or steamed vegetables, or a simple vegetable soup.
- Each day, aim to have one fruit meal, one meal planned around a protein main dish and one meal planned around a starch main dish.
- Make one, or both, of these meals (the protein and carbohydrate meals) a salad meal, too, served with raw vegetables.
- You can always increase the number of fruit meals. For instance, you could have fruit for, say, breakfast and lunch, for faster weight-loss, and have some days when you only eat fruit.

• If this seems complicated, start by always having fruit for breakfast, a large salad for lunch, and *either* a carbohydrate or protein evening meal with lots of cooked or raw vegetables.

• You can have 300 ml/10 fl oz (½ pint) skimmed milk each day for use in drinks. It's really best not to have drinks with milk in them when you are eating carbohydrate meals, although if the quantity of milk is small, you can probably get away with it.

Meals suitable for vegans are marked Ⓥ, but please read vegan margarine (such as Vitaquell) for butter.

Meals for the Vegetarian Hip and Thigh Diet (see page 152) are marked ⒣.

FRUIT MEALS, FOR BREAKFAST, LUNCH OR EVENING – ALL Ⓥ, ALL ⒣

Have at least one of these each day, preferably for breakfast. You can also have fresh fruit juices with your fruit meals. Try:

2–3 mellow apples
2 bananas
a bunch of grapes
a wedge of melon
2–3 peaches
a baked apple stuffed with raisins or sultanas, no sugar or butter
a bowl of cherries
any fresh fruit, or mixture of fruit, no sugar
Apple, Grape and Orange Fruit Salad (page 240)
Mango, Kiwi and Pawpaw Fruit Salad (page 240)

122

Strawberry, Grape and Kiwi Fruit Salad (page 241)
Pear, Grape and Orange Fruit Salad (page 241)
Strawberry and Orange Fruit Salad (page 241)

BREAKFASTS

If you don't want to have fruit for breakfast, have fruit or fruit and vegetables for lunch or the evening meal instead, and choose one of these, either carbohydrate or protein, for breakfast:

CARBOHYDRATE

BAKED POTATO Ⓥ, ⒣

A 225 g/8 oz baked potato served with 7 g/¼ oz butter, no cheese

CROISSANT

1 warm croissant, with 7 g/¼ oz butter if liked

WHOLEMEAL TOAST AND HONEY Ⓥ

2 pieces of wholemeal toast, 7 g/¼ oz butter, 2 teaspoons honey

WARM ROLL AND HONEY Ⓥ

Warm wholemeal roll, 7 g/¼ oz butter, 2 teaspoons honey

BANANA MUESLI Ⓥ, ⒣

Muesli made from 25 g/1 oz rolled oats moistened with water, mixed with 1 sliced banana and 1 tablespoon raisins

PORRIDGE Ⓥ, ⒽⓉ

Stir 25 g/1 oz rolled oats and 150 ml/5 fl oz water
in a pan over a medium heat for 2 minutes until
thickened. Serve with 1 teaspoon honey or brown
sugar and 1 tablespoon cream (optional)

PROTEIN

YOGURT, FRUIT AND HONEY ⒽⓉ

150 ml/5 fl oz plain unsweetened yogurt with 1
teaspoon honey and 1 large chopped apple or pear

GRAPEFRUIT; MUSHROOM OMELETTE

½ grapefruit, or grapefruit and orange segments;
Mushroom Omelette (page 217)

GRAPEFRUIT; GOAT'S CHEESE ON TOMATOES

½ grapefruit; Goat's Cheese on Tomato Slices (see
page 221)

TOFU WHIZZ Ⓥ, ⒽⓉ

The night before, put 225 g/8 oz strawberries or other soft
fruit, peeled and sliced, into the freezer. Next day, put
the fruit into a food processor with ½ × 275 g/10 oz
packet silken tofu and 1–2 teaspoons honey, and whizz to
a thick, smooth purée. You can use bought frozen strawberries for this as long as they do not contain extra sugar.
Let them thaw at room temperature for 15 minutes before
use.

GRAPEFRUIT OR ORANGE JUICE; TOFU GRILL (V), (HT)

½ grapefruit, or a glass of orange juice

Cut ½ × 275 g/10 oz packet smoked or marinated firm tofu into thin slices and heat under the grill or in a microwave. Serve with grilled tomatoes and mushrooms fried in 1 teaspoon olive oil or melted butter.

SCRAMBLED EGGS; TOMATOES AND MUSHROOMS

Scramble 2 eggs with 2–3 tablespoons milk and 7 g/¼ oz butter. Serve with grilled tomatoes and mushrooms fried in 1 teaspoon olive oil or melted butter.

LUNCHES/EVENING MEALS

For either of these meals you can always have fruit, chosen from the Fruit Meals (page 122). Otherwise, choose either a vegetable, protein or carbohydrate meal, according to what else you are eating that day.

VEGETABLE (OR VEGETABLE AND FRUIT) MEALS

AUBERGINE WITH SOY AND GINGER; STIR-FRIED BEANSPROUTS, CARROTS AND GREEN PEPPER; FRUIT (V), (HT)

Aubergine with Soy and Ginger (page 187), served with Stir-Fried Beansprouts, Carrots and Green Pepper (page 190); any fresh fruit.

SPICED VEGETABLES; SLICED TOMATOES AND ONIONS Ⓥ, ⒣⒯

Serve the Spiced Vegetables (page 189) with a salad of sliced tomatoes and onions.

RATATOUILLE; SALAD; ANY FRUIT Ⓥ, ⒣⒯

Ratatouille (page 197), with a salad of chopped lettuce, onion and watercress (and a few dandelion leaves if available), and a piece of fruit. The salad can be dressed with a little oil and cider vinegar or lemon juice, in which case choose fruit from the list of those which go with protein meals (pages 119–120).

VEGETABLE GOULASH; GREEN BEANS OR WATERCRESS Ⓥ, ⒣⒯

Vegetable Goulash (page 198), with cooked green beans, or watercress.

AVOCADO SALAD; FRUIT Ⓥ

½ large avocado dressed with lemon juice, salt and black pepper, with a salad of lettuce, skinned and sliced tomato, cucumber and sliced onion. To follow, any fruit chosen from those which go with protein meals.

The following suggestions also make good packed lunches:

COLESLAW; FRESH FRUIT Ⓥ, ⒣⒯

Coleslaw (page 159), or Creamy Coleslaw (page 160), with any fruit chosen from those which go with protein meals. (The lemon juice, vinegar and/or yogurt in the dressing would not go with a carbohydrate fruit.)

FENNEL, RED PEPPER AND CARROT SALAD; FRUIT (V), (HT)

Fennel, Red Pepper and Carrot Salad (page 160); with any fruit chosen from those which go with protein meals.

HERBS AND FLOWERS SALAD; FRUIT (V), (HT)

Herbs and Flowers Salad (page 163); with any fruit chosen from those which go with protein meals. Alternatively have the Lettuce and Nasturtium Flower Salad (page 164) or the Cucumber, Raspberry and Rose Petal Salad (page 162).

CABBAGE, APPLE AND SAGE SALAD; FRUIT (V), (HT)

Cabbage, Apple and Sage Salad (page 163); with any fruit chosen from those which go with protein meals, or a large glass of freshly squeezed orange juice.

FIVE-STAR SALAD OR MAIN-COURSE SALAD; FRUIT (V), (HT)

Five-Star Salad (page 165) or Main-Course Salad (page 166), with any fruit chosen from those which go with protein meals.

AVOCADO AND SALAD (V)

Good as a packed lunch: halve 1 small ripe avocado, remove stone, sprinkle inside with lemon juice, add salt and freshly ground black pepper, put two halves back together again and wrap well. Pack a teaspoon, and a salad of lettuce, watercress, cucumber and carrot sticks.

HEARTY VEGETABLE SOUP; FRESH LETTUCE, CUCUMBER STICKS OR CRESS; FRUIT Ⓥ, ⒽⓉ

Hearty Vegetable Soup (page 174); small salad of lettuce, cucumber sticks or cress; any fruit.

ROOT VEGETABLE SOUP; CELERY STICKS; FRUIT Ⓥ, ⒽⓉ

Root Vegetable Soup (page 172), served with celery sticks and any fruit chosen from those which go with protein meals. Alternatively, have the Curried Tomato and Apple Soup (page 173).

MUSHROOM PÂTÉ; RAW VEGETABLES; FRUIT Ⓥ, ⒽⓉ

Serve the Mushroom Pâté (page 181), with raw vegetables for dipping – carrot sticks, cauliflower florets, radishes, or whatever is available. Finish with any fresh fruit.

CARBOHYDRATE MEALS

AUBERGINE WITH SOY AND GINGER; STIR-FRIED BEANSPROUTS; CARROTS AND GREEN PEPPER; BROWN RICE; SLICED BANANA WITH CHOPPED GINGER Ⓥ, ⒽⓉ

Aubergine with Soy and Ginger (page 187), served with Stir-Fried Beansprouts, Carrots and Green Pepper (page 190) and 100 g/4 oz cooked brown rice, followed by a banana sliced and topped with a piece of crystallised or preserved ginger, chopped.

SPICED VEGETABLES; BROWN RICE; SLICED TOMATOES AND ONIONS Ⓥ, ⒽⓉ

Serve the Spiced Vegetables (page 189), with 100 g/4 oz cooked brown rice and a salad of sliced tomatoes and onions.

BAKED POTATO; BUTTER; SALAD; RIPE PEAR Ⓥ, ⒽⓉ

A 225 g/8 oz potato, served with 7 g/¼ oz butter, and a large salad made from lettuce, grated carrot, sliced cucumber, sliced tomato, celery, and any chopped fresh herbs available. Follow with a ripe pear if liked.

GARLIC BREAD AND SALAD Ⓥ

Salad of lettuce, peeled and sliced tomatoes, onion rings and a few black olives. Serve with 2 slices of granary stick spread with 15 g/½ oz butter which has been mixed with ½ garlic clove, crushed, then grilled until the butter is melted and the bread is heated through and crisp.

SOUP; GARLIC BREAD; CELERY AND CUCUMBER STICKS Ⓥ

Carrot Soup (page 176), or Potato and Onion Soup (page 175), or Watercress Soup (page 176), with garlic bread made as above and some celery and cucumber sticks.

BAKED POTATO WITH SOURED CREAM AND ASPARAGUS; SALAD ⒽⓉ

Baked Potato with Soured Cream and Asparagus (page 200), with whatever salad you fancy – lettuce, tomatoes, grated carrot, watercress – but no dressing.

SLIMMERS' CHIPS; GRATED CARROT, LETTUCE AND WATERCRESS Ⓥ, ⒣⒯

Slimmers' Chips (page 201), with a large salad of grated carrot, lettuce and watercress (no dressing).

SWEETCORN POTATO; TOMATO, CUCUMBER, PEPPER AND ONION SALAD Ⓥ, ⒣⒯

Sweetcorn Potato (page 201); salad of chopped tomato, cucumber, green pepper and onion (no dressing).

ONION BAKED POTATO; VEGETABLES OR SALAD Ⓥ, ⒣⒯

Onion Baked Potato (page 202), with all the vegetables you want, and/or a large salad, dressed with rice vinegar and oil.

QUICK VEGETABLE HOTPOT; SLICED PEAR WITH CINNAMON, AND CREAM IF LIKED Ⓥ, ⒣⒯

Quick Vegetable Hotpot (page 200), with a side salad if liked (celery and watercress); peeled and sliced pear, topped with 1 tablespoon single cream if liked, and a sprinkling of cinnamon.

FETTUCINE WITH RED PEPPER; LEAFY SALAD Ⓥ

Fettucine with Red Pepper (page 222), and a salad of mixed leaves as available: lettuce, dandelion, chicory, radicchio, or a ready-washed continental leaf salad from a supermarket (no dressing).

PARSLEY POTATO CAKES; COOKED CARROTS AND PEAS Ⓥ, Ⓗᴛ

Parsley Potato Cakes (page 204), with cooked carrots and peas.

CREAMY POTATO BAKE; COOKED BROCCOLI OR SALAD Ⓗᴛ

Creamy Potato Bake (page 204), with cooked broccoli or a salad of grated carrot, red pepper rings and watercress (no dressing).

TAGLIATELLE WITH CREAM AND BROCCOLI; TOMATO SALAD

Tagliatelle with Cream and Broccoli (page 224); salad of skinned, sliced tomatoes with chopped spring onions. Alternatively, make Tagliatelle with Asparagus (page 224) or Tagliatelle with Spring Vegetables (page 224).

FETTUCINE WITH MUSHROOMS IN CREAM SAUCE; MIXED SALAD

Fettucine with Mushrooms in Cream Sauce (page 222); with a mixed salad of lettuce, tomato, cucumber and green pepper (no dressing).

FRENCH ONION QUICHE; MIXED SALAD

Make the French Onion Quiche (page 214) using 2 egg yolks instead of a whole egg. (Or make the Broccoli, Mushroom or Leek variations.) Serve with a mixed salad of curly endive, radicchio, lamb's lettuce and escarole, or a ready-washed continental leaf salad from a supermarket (no dressing).

GREEK SPINACH PIE; TOMATO, CUCUMBER, ONION, GREEN PEPPER AND BLACK OLIVE SALAD Ⓥ

Greek Spinach Pie (page 216), with a salad of chopped tomatoes, cucumber, onion, green pepper and a few black olives.

BROWN RICE WITH MUSHROOMS IN CREAM; TOMATO AND BASIL SALAD Ⓗⓣ

Brown Rice with Mushrooms in Cream (page 230), with a salad of skinned, sliced tomatoes sprinkled with chopped basil if available.

MASHED POTATOES; SALAD Ⓗⓣ

225 g/8 oz potatoes mashed with some of the cooking water, a little butter and 1 tablespoon single cream instead of milk (which would be incompatible with the carbohydrate); large salad of lettuce or endive, grated carrot and sliced, skinned tomato.

COMPATIBLE PIZZA; SALAD Ⓥ

Homemade pizza: fry an onion, some red pepper and mushrooms in 1 teaspoon olive oil until tender; arrange on top of a round pitta bread, top with 1 tablespoon frozen sweetcorn kernels or 4 black olives, then bake or grill for 15–20 minutes, to heat through. Serve with lettuce and cucumber salad.

The following suggestions also make good packed lunches:

HEARTY VEGETABLE SOUP; WARM GRANARY ROLL; SALAD ⓥ

Hearty Vegetable Soup (page 174); serve with a warm granary roll and a lettuce and watercress salad (no dressing). This makes a good packed lunch if you put the soup in a thermos.

MUSHROOM PÂTÉ; TOAST; SALAD; RIPE PEAR ⓥ

Serve the Mushroom Pâté (page 181), with 1–2 slices of wholemeal toast, 7 g/¼ oz butter and any raw vegetables you choose – some grated carrot on lettuce leaves, sprinkled with mustard and cress is good. Finish with a ripe pear if you wish. This makes a good packed lunch if you use Melba toast or 4 crispbreads instead of the toast.

MARMITE AND CUCUMBER SANDWICH; WATERCRESS, TOMATO AND/OR LETTUCE; BANANA OR RIPE PEAR ⓥ

Marmite and Cucumber Sandwich (page 169), with as much tomato and/or lettuce as you like, and a ripe banana or pear to finish, if liked.

CREAMY CARROT SANDWICH; LETTUCE, TOMATO AND CUCUMBER

Creamy Carrot Sandwich (page 170), with cucumber, tomato and lettuce. This makes a convenient packed lunch.

MUSHROOM PÂTÉ SANDWICH; CELERY STICKS ⓥ

The Mushroom Pâté Sandwich (page 170), with celery sticks.

SALAD SANDWICH; BANANA ⓥ

Salad Sandwich (page 170), with a ripe banana.

SALAD-FILLED PITTA BREAD ⓥ

Slit a wholemeal pitta bread and fill with a mixture of chopped lettuce, tomatoes, onion, cucumber, sprouted seeds if you have them, grated carrot. Dress with salt, pepper and 1 teaspoon olive oil (no lemon or vinegar), or use 1 tablespoon soured cream for a dressing.

CREAMY CARROT AND CHINESE LEAVES SALAD; CRISPS

Make a salad by mixing coarsely grated carrot, shredded Chinese leaves and chopped green pepper with 1 tablespoon soured cream per person. Serve with 25 g/1 oz crisps, any flavour.

PROTEIN MEALS

HERBS AND FLOWERS SALAD; GOAT'S CHEESE OR CURD CHEESE; FRUIT ⓗⓣ

Herbs and Flowers Salad (page 163), served with 50 g/2 oz thinly sliced goat's cheese or 100 g/4 oz curd cheese. Any fruit chosen from those which go with protein meals. Alternatively have the Lettuce and Nasturtium Flower Salad (page 164); or the Cucumber, Raspberry and Rose Petal Salad (page 162).

CITRUS-MARINATED TOFU WITH STIR-FRIED VEGETABLES; AUBERGINE WITH SOY AND GINGER; FRUIT Ⓥ, ⒣

Citrus-Marinated Tofu with Stir-Fried Vegetables (page 192); Aubergine with Soy and Ginger (page 187); any fresh fruit chosen from those that go with protein meals.

SPICED VEGETABLES; SLICED TOMATOES AND ONIONS; RAITA ⒣

Serve the Spiced Vegetables (page 189), with a salad of sliced tomatoes and onions, and raita made with 150 ml/5 fl oz plain low-fat yogurt and 2.5 cm/1 in cucumber, chopped.

RATATOUILLE WITH FLAKED ALMONDS; FRENCH BEANS; BAKED APPLE Ⓥ, ⒣

Ratatouille (page 197), with 40 g/1½ oz flaked almonds per serving; steamed French beans and a baked apple stuffed with raisins.

GOAT'S CHEESE ON TOMATO SLICES; CABBAGE, APPLE AND SAGE SALAD ⒣

Serve the Goat's Cheese on Tomato Slices (page 221) with the Cabbage, Apple and Sage Salad (page 163).

SPINACH ROULADE; PEAS AND CARROTS; CONTINENTAL LEAF SALAD ⒣

Spinach Roulade (page 220), with cooked peas and carrots, and a salad made from continental leaves tossed in a light dressing of lemon juice and a little olive oil.

GRATIN OF VEGETABLES; TOMATO AND LETTUCE SALAD; STEWED DRIED APRICOTS WITH CHOPPED ALMONDS Ⓗ

Lightly cook a selection of any vegetables except potatoes, allowing about 350 g/12 oz per person. Put the cooked vegetables into a shallow casserole and sprinkle with 50 g/2 oz grated cheese per person. Grill until the cheese is melted and lightly browned. Serve with a salad made from skinned and sliced tomatoes and shredded lettuce. Follow with some fresh or stewed dried apricots topped with 2 teaspoons flaked almonds.

MUSHROOM, HERB, ASPARAGUS OR TOMATO OMELETTE; SPINACH OR OTHER GREEN SALAD Ⓗ

Mushroom, herb, asparagus or tomato Omelette (page 217), with a salad made by finely shredding tender raw spinach and dressing it with crushed garlic, lemon juice and a little olive oil.

VEGETABLE STIR-FRY WITH MARINATED TOFU; WHITE AND RED CABBAGE SALAD Ⓥ, Ⓗ

Vegetable Stir-Fry with Marinated Tofu (page 191), served with a salad made by shredding white and red cabbage thinly, mixing together, and tossing in a little olive oil and lemon juice.

LENTIL DAL; STEAMED BRUSSELS SPROUTS; SLICED TOMATOES AND ONION RINGS Ⓥ, ⒣Ⓣ

Lentil Dal (page 206), with halved and steamed brussels sprouts, and a salad of sliced tomatoes and onion rings.

BUTTERBEANS BAKED WITH A HERBY TOPPING; SPRING CABBAGE; TOMATO SALAD Ⓥ

Butterbeans Baked with a Herby Topping (page 206), using the wheatgerm variation, with cooked spring cabbage and skinned and sliced tomatoes.

EASY CHILLI; STEAMED BROCCOLI Ⓥ, ⒣Ⓣ

Easy Chilli (page 210), with steamed broccoli.

CANNELLINI BEAN, ONION AND GARLIC STEW; PURPLE SPROUTING BROCCOLI; FRESH FRUIT SALAD Ⓥ, ⒣Ⓣ

Cannellini Bean, Onion and Garlic Stew (page 207); lightly cooked purple sprouting broccoli; fruit salad made from ½ orange, ½ apple, ½ kiwi fruit and 50 g/2 oz black grapes, with 1 tablespoon single cream if liked.

VEGETABLE GOULASH; LETTUCE AND CUCUMBER SALAD Ⓥ, ⒣Ⓣ

Vegetable Goulash (page 198); salad of crisp lettuce leaves and thinly sliced cucumber sprinkled with chopped dill or parsley if available.

The following suggestions also make good packed lunches:

NUTTY COLESLAW; APPLE Ⓥ, ⒣ⓣ

Nutty Coleslaw (page 159), or Cheesy Coleslaw (page 160), with an apple.

GREEK SALAD; SLICED PEACHES ⒣ⓣ

Greek Salad (page 160); Sliced Peaches.

FIVE-STAR SALAD OR MAIN-COURSE SALAD; GREEK YOGURT AND FRUIT ⒣ⓣ

Five-Star Salad (page 165) or Main-Course Salad (page 166), followed by Greek yogurt with sliced apple and a few raisins.

FENNEL, RED PEPPER AND CARROT SALAD; CURD OR COTTAGE CHEESE; APPLE, ORANGE OR SATSUMA ⒣ⓣ

Fennel, Red Pepper and Carrot Salad (page 160); with 75 g/3 oz curd or cottage cheese, and an apple, orange or satsuma.

LENTIL SOUP; CUCUMBER, CELERY AND CARROT STICKS Ⓥ, ⒣ⓣ

Lentil Soup (page 174), with cucumber, celery and carrot sticks.

TSATSIKI; SPRING ONIONS, SLICED GREEN AND RED PEPPERS; APPLE ⒣ⓣ

Tsatsiki (page 181), with a salad made from spring onions, and sliced green and red peppers; an apple.

HUMMUS WITH RAW VEGETABLES Ⓥ, Ⓗⓣ

Hummus (page 182), with plenty of raw vegetables for dipping: cauliflower florets, carrot sticks, strips of red pepper, celery, cucumber.

HEARTY VEGETABLE SOUP; GREEK YOGURT AND APPLE Ⓗⓣ

Hearty Vegetable Soup (page 174); Greek yogurt and slices of apple.

ROOT VEGETABLE SOUP; STILTON CHEESE WITH CELERY STICKS AND APPLE Ⓗⓣ

Root Vegetable Soup (page 172); 50 g/2 oz Stilton cheese with celery sticks and an apple, preferably a Cox.

HARDBOILED EGG AND SALAD; FRESH FRUIT Ⓗⓣ

1 hardboiled egg; lettuce, tomato and cucumber salad; any fruit chosen from those which go with protein meals.

COTTAGE OR CURD CHEESE AND CRUDITÉS; FRESH FRUIT Ⓗⓣ

100 g/4 oz cottage or curd cheese; carrot, celery and cucumber sticks; any fresh fruit chosen from those which go with protein meals.

139

MIXED BEAN SALAD; LETTUCE AND WATERCRESS; APPLE OR ORANGE Ⓥ, ⒣ⓣ

Make a salad by mixing ½ × 400 g/14 oz can drained mixed beans with 1 tablespoon chopped onion, a squeeze of lemon juice and 1 teaspoon olive oil. Serve with lettuce and watercress, and an apple or orange (or other fruit chosen from those which go with protein meals).

NUTS AND SALAD Ⓥ, ⒣ⓣ

50 g/2 oz fresh shelled nuts: almonds, walnuts, pecans, Brazils; salad of cucumber wedges.

CHEDDAR CHEESE AND MIXED SALAD; COX APPLE

50 g/2 oz matured Cheddar cheese with a salad of lettuce, tomato, spring onions, cucumber and celery; Cox apple.

SAMPLE MENUS

These sample menus show how you can plan your menus in practice. Ⓕⓥ means fruit and vegetable meal; Ⓒ means carbohydrate; Ⓟ means protein.

BREAKFAST	LUNCH	EVENING MEAL
Apples Ⓕⓥ	Herbs and Flowers Salad (page 163) Goat's cheese Ⓟ Grapes	Baked potatoes with butter Ⓒ Salad Ripe pear

Wholemeal Toast and Honey (page 123) ©️	Lentil Soup (page 174) ℗️ Cucumber, celery and carrot sticks	Spiced Vegetables (page 189) 🄵🅅 Sliced tomato and onion
Melon 🄵🅅	Salad Sandwich (page 170) ©️ Banana	Gratin of Vegetables (page 196) ℗️ Tomato and lettuce Stewed dried apricots
Bananas 🄵🅅	Coleslaw (page 159) 🄵🅅 Fresh fruit	Fettucine with Mushrooms in Cream Sauce (page 223) ©️ Mixed salad
Scrambled Eggs (page 125) ℗️ Tomatoes and mushrooms	Five-Star Salad (page 165) 🄵🅅 Apple	Creamy Potato Bake (page 204) ©️ Broccoli
Mango 🄵🅅	Avocado and Salad (page 127) 🄵🅅	Compatible Pizza (page 132) ©️ Salad
Apples 🄵🅅	Carrot Soup (page 176) with Garlic Bread (page 129) ©️ Celery and cucumber	Vegetable Stir-Fry with Marinated Tofu (page 191) ℗️

ADAPTING THE DIET

IF YOU'RE COOKING FOR A FAMILY . . .

This is not a difficult diet to adapt to the needs of a family. Many of the dishes are popular, but unless your family want to eat compatibly along with you, they may like extras added. For instance, they might like to have bread, pasta, potatoes or rice with a protein meal, grated cheese or other protein with a carbohydrate meal, and a non-compatible pudding. The menu suggestions given can easily be boosted in this way.

IF YOU'RE A VEGAN . . .

A number of the meals suggested in this food-combining diet are marked Ⓥ, and many of the recipes in this book are also vegan as they stand or in one of their variations. These too are marked Ⓥ.

IF YOU'RE COOKING FOR ONE . . .

You are in an ideal position to follow a compatible-eating diet. If you haven't much time for cooking or don't feel like making complicated meals, you can choose some of the simple menu suggestions. There are also lunch box ideas in each section for eating at work, or for simple meals at home.

Business lunches need not be a problem, either, and in some ways are made easier by the fact that you know you can only eat certain foods together. You may need to be prepared to talk about your diet, though! Follow the guidance given under Eating Out (page 145); eat lightly, and if necessary, have fruit both for breakfast and in the evening (or one of the fruit and vegetable suggestions given on pages 125–132).

IF YOU'RE AN OLDER PERSON . . .

You could find compatible eating particularly beneficial, especially if you have digestive difficulties. Indigestion often goes as if by magic, along with the excess weight; arthritic pains and stiffness usually ease or disappear; and allergies, chronic migraine and hay fever are often quickly resolved. Doris Grant, leading exponent of the Hay System, puts this down to the fact that when you combine foods properly the body is more able to use its regenerative healing powers.

If you don't like eating a great many salads or raw vegetables, consider taking these in the form of juice; or have one of the vegetable soups, or lightly cooked vegetables, for your fruit and vegetable meal.

IF YOU'RE PREGNANT . . .

Slimming is not advisable when you are pregnant. However this food-combining diet is a healthy way of eating, and you could follow this diet, allowing yourself unrestricted quantities of foods, and making sure that you have at least one protein meal each day. If you have digestive problems, you will probably find that these are eased by eating compatibly.

IF YOU'RE COOKING FOR CHILDREN . . .

See the section on page 99.

FAST FOODS, TAKEAWAYS AND CONVENIENCE FOODS

It's quite possible to get fast foods which are suitable for a food-combining diet, but sometimes you need to ask for special versions. For instance, plain salad sandwiches without cheese or egg; a ploughman's lunch with *either* the bread *or* the cheese; a baked potato with just butter or soured cream and salad, no cheese. Although, strictly speaking, cooked tomatoes do not combine well with carbohydrate, a pizza without any cheese is another possibility which you might consider having occasionally. Vegetable curries, birianis and pilaus are all usually suitable, as are Chinese stir-fried vegetables with rice. Chips, with a salad, provide another possibility.

When buying convenience foods, you should always read the labels to make sure that proteins and carbohydrates have not been mixed together. It's surprising how often flour, for instance, creeps into a protein dish, or skimmed milk powder, albumen (egg white) or whey into a carbohydrate one. Meals planned for vegans can often be a better bet than vegetarian ones, since these do not contain any dairy products, but, even so, you need to read the labels carefully.

EATING OUT

When you eat out, the choice is more limited than usual, since many vegetarian dishes mix proteins and carbohydrates. It's often easiest to opt for a carbohydrate meal, unless you choose the ubiquitous omelette, with cooked vegetables and/or a salad, not chips. On the other hand, chips (or new or baked potatoes) on their own would be all right, with a salad or cooked vegetables as you wish.

The best first courses to choose are cooked vegetables, or salads; artichoke, asparagus or, before a carbohydrate meal, corn on the cob, or garlic mushrooms, or mushrooms à la Grecque. A clear vegetable soup (made without meat or fish stock, of course) is fine, as is a simple vegetable soup, which can be thickened with potato if you are going to follow it with a carbohydrate main course, too. Garlic bread is all right before a carbohydrate main course, too.

For the main course, many pasta dishes are suitable, as long as they do not contain cheese. You might find yourself having to have spaghetti Napolitana, which is all right occasionally, although not perfect because of the mismatch of cooked tomatoes and carbohydrate, and the same applies with pizza, as mentioned above. Nevertheless, pizza without cheese is something you could have occasionally when eating out.

Indian meals are good from the combining point of view, but they contain an awful lot of oil and it's so easy to eat too much! Middle Eastern food can be a good choice but you'll need to decide whether to opt for a carbohydrate meal, which enables you to enjoy the delicious breads and rice dishes, or for a protein one in which you can include goat's cheese, yogurt dishes and pulses, including hummus. Chinese vegetarian dishes are good, but, again, stick to *either* rice *or* protein dishes (including eggs or tofu) to keep your meal compatible. If you opt for rice you could have some sake, too (being rice-based, it's also compatible!).

It's safest to bypass the puddings when you're eating compatibly, although you could have fruit salad or a sorbet after a protein meal and vanilla ice-cream made from cream and egg yolks, or a crème caramel (if it's made with egg yolks) after a carbohydrate meal. Perhaps this isn't the best way to lose weight, though! If you opt for coffee instead of a dessert, you could allow yourself some cream in it for a treat, or take your own sachet of herbal tea and just ask for hot water, if you prefer.

ENTERTAINING

It isn't difficult to put together some delicious compatible menus. When planning a meal, decide first whether you want to make it a protein or carbohydrate meal. A protein meal is often more convenient for entertaining because it enables you to have some wine. You can either give your guests a completely compatible meal, which may intrigue and interest them, or you might prefer to offer them some extras, such as bread or rolls with their vegetable soup before a protein meal. Your decision will probably depend on the occasion, and the guests! Here are some suggestions based on recipes in this book.

SUMMER LUNCH Ⓟ

Chilled Cucumber and Yogurt Soup (page 177)
Ratatouille (page 197)
Herbs and Flowers Salad (page 163)
Strawberries and cream

WINTER LUNCH Ⓟ, Ⓥ

Root Vegetable Soup (page 172)
Stuffed Aubergines (page 199)
Aniseed Carrots (page 186)
Salad of continental leaves with vinaigrette dressing
Pears in Wine (page 239)

WITH A FRENCH FLAVOUR Ⓒ

Watercress Soup (page 176) with warm poppyseed rolls
Brown Rice with Mushrooms in Cream (page 230)
French beans
Tomato salad with chopped fresh basil
Ripe grapes

Ⓒ

Mushroom Pâté (page 181) with Melba toast
French Onion Quiche (page 214)
Mangetout and baby carrots
Watercress and sliced radishes
Fresh, very ripe pawpaw

WITH AN ITALIAN FLAVOUR Ⓒ, Ⓥ

Globe Artichokes (page 183)
Fettucine with Red Pepper (page 222)
Salad of continental leaves with sliced red onion rings
Fresh figs

WITH A GREEK FLAVOUR ⓟ

Tsatsiki (page 181)
Aubergine Bake (page 195)
Greek Salad (page 160) or salad of mixed leaves
Watermelon

WITH AN INDIAN FLAVOUR ⓟ, ⓥ

Curried Tomato and Apple Soup (page 173)
Spiced Vegetables (page 189)
Lentil Dal (page 206)
Tomato and onion salad

WITH AN ORIENTAL FLAVOUR ⓟ, ⓥ

Miso Broth (page 177)
Vegetable Stir-Fry with Marinated Tofu (page 191)
Orange, Kiwi and Lychee Fruit Salad (page 240)

COOKING FOR A CROWD ⓒ, ⓥ

Mushroom Risotto (page 228)
Baked potatoes
Salad of mixed leaves and chopped fresh herbs, dressed
with a little oil, no lemon or vinegar
Pears with chopped crystallised ginger

ⓟ, ⓥ

Provençal Stew (page 194)
Green salad with garlic dressing
Pineapple and Orange Sorbet (page 234) or Peaches in
Wine (page 239)

CAN YOU DRINK WHEN FOOD-COMBINING?

As you will see from the chart on page 282, beer and lager combine with carbohydrate meals, whilst wine and cider (being fruit-based) combine with protein meals, and also with fruit and vegetable meals. Whisky is neutral. However, drinking and losing weight do not go easily together, whatever diet you're using. So even compatible drinks are best limited to the occasional celebratory glass. Slimline mixers are not recommended in any system of compatible eating. If you want to drink fruit juice, choose one which combines well with the type of meal you are having. For instance, apple, grapefruit or orange juice go with a protein meal, and grape juice with a carbohydrate meal, although you shouldn't drink too much fruit juice, either, if you want to lose weight quickly! Natural or sparkling spring water is the best bet, with a twist of lemon or lime if you're drinking it with a protein meal.

THE QUICK FRUIT CLEANSING DIET

One of the best ways of shedding a few pounds quickly, and cleansing your system at the same time, is to have a day or two eating only fruit. No matter what nutritionists and food scientists say, there do seem to be certain fruits which are more helpful than others when you are trying to lose weight. Pineapple is excellent – see the Pineapple and Banana Diet (page 115) – also pawpaws, mangoes, apples, watermelon, grapes and strawberries. You need to eat watermelon or grapes for the whole day to get the maximum benefit, weight-wise, and a whole day on apples and mangoes also works well. If you wish, you can have up to three different types of fruits during the day, but don't eat them together, and allow a 2- or 3-hour interval between eating each type.

Prunes soaked in boiling water for 1 hour before you eat them, followed (at least 2 hours later) by strawberries, is a particularly cleansing combination. Have 2 bananas late at night to soothe your system after this. If you have already had a day on fruit and feel hungry the next morning, start the day with 2 bananas and then go on to other fruits after at least 2 hours: maybe dried apricots, prunes or strawberries, with cherries or blueberries to end the day. Drink pure water and clear herb tea or weak clear China tea (no milk, sugar, sweeteners, lemon juice or coffee).

A day or two on fruits will help you to break old eating habits and lose a bit of weight quickly. Choose a weekend, or a couple of days when you know you will be able to take things easy and won't have to cook food for other people. You may feel a little tired in the evening, so be prepared to pamper yourself and go to bed early, with a good book or some music to listen to. After your cleansing days, move on to one of the long-term diets – the Vegetarian Slimming Plan for Calorie-Counters or Food-Combiners or the Vegetarian Hip and Thigh Diet.

COMING OFF THE DIET AND STAYING SLIM

Once you get used to food-combining, it feels so good that you want to go on with it! This is a diet which many people find can easily become a permanent way of eating, and you may find that your weight naturally stabilises at a level which feels good. Some people find that although they go a little below their goal weight initially, they put a little weight back on again and then remain at this level without apparently changing their diet. If you want to lose more, you can simply increase the number of fruit days and fruit lunches you have; and on other days, try to make sure that one of your meals is based on vegetables or a single carbohydrate. If you want to gain weight, just do the opposite. Have fewer fruit days, fruit lunches and light meals. (See page 115 for more tips on staying slim.)

Sometimes you may feel that you want to break the rules and have a meal which is not properly combined, like a cheese sandwich or scrambled eggs on toast. That's fine; have what you fancy and notice how you feel afterwards. Of course, if you wish to eat 'normally' after losing weight on this food-combining diet, that's all right, too. But keep an eye on your weight and have a few days of food-combining, or on the Quick Fruit Cleansing Diet (page 149), or the Rice and Fruit Diet (page 113), to get rid of any extra pounds quickly and keep slim and healthy.

THE VEGETARIAN HIP AND THIGH DIET

Many people have found that a diet low in fat is particularly helpful for removing the obstinate fat which lingers stubbornly around the hips and thighs. Because it contains no saturated fat and has a high proportion of cleansing fresh fruit and vegetables, a vegetarian slimming diet is naturally helpful in shifting weight from the hips and thighs, as well as solving that other related problem, cellulite. A low-fat vegetarian diet rich in fresh fruit and vegetables (with as many raw as possible) and low in wheat and dairy produce, combined with gentle exercise and massage with aromatherapy oils, can work wonders with lumpy, cellulite-ridden hips and thighs. Here's how.

HOW THE DIET WORKS

A few days on a cleansing diet will get you off to a good start. The Pineapple and Banana Diet (page 115), followed by 2–3 days on the Quick Fruit Cleansing Diet (page 149), will help you to lose a few pounds quickly and get rid of toxins. Or you could follow the Rice and Fruit Diet (page 113), for up to two weeks, for excellent weight-loss and general cleansing. During this time, avoid alcohol, and you'll get best results if you also avoid smoking and drinking coffee. Have weak tea – no milk – and a cup of fennel tea (see page 65) three times a day.

After this period of cleansing, follow the food-combining diet, choosing only those menus and recipes marked (HT). These menus and recipes do not contain wheat products, and only have limited amounts of cow's milk or cow's-milk products. Goat's milk, and goat's-milk cheese and yogurt (or sheep's-milk yogurt) are better than cow's-milk products.

Make sure your diet is high in raw fruit and vegetables by making breakfast a meal based on fresh fruit, and in addition make one of the other main meals of the day a fruit and vegetable meal, preferably a large salad, such as the Five-Star Salad (page 165), with fresh fruit to follow. Then, for your other meal of the day, choose either a protein or a carbohydrate menu from those marked (HT), or select a main-course dish from the recipe section, choosing those marked with the (HT) symbol.

EXERCISE, SKIN-BRUSHING AND MASSAGE

The simple stretching, bending and toning routine (page 46), or the slimmer's yoga routine (page 50), will help to tone up your hips and thighs. In addition, the skin-brushing described on page 71 will help to draw out impurities through the skin and to improve the circulation. Aromatherapy oils can help cellulite, as described on page 67. You might consider having an aromatherapy treatment, and then using the oils suggested in your bath afterwards, or making up a massage oil yourself using 10 ml/2 teaspoons pure almond oil with geranium, bergamot, fennel and cyprus, all together, or in various combinations, to make 6 drops in all. Vary the combinations and the exact amounts as described on page 67. Or use one of the anti-cellulite oils you can buy in chemists and beauty departments. Really massage the oil into your skin, pinching, pummelling and kneading the flesh. But remember to love your body rather than hate it, as you visualise the cellulite and fat dispersing!

Part 3
The Recipes

~~~~~

NOTES ON INGREDIENTS

Most of the ingredients used in this book are readily available. One or two are more unusual but you should be able to get them at healthfood shops.

BUTTER

Where a solid fat is used, I prefer to use *small* quantities of butter rather than either margarine or low-fat spreads. If you want to use a margarine, I recommend Vitaquell, from healthfood shops.

CHILLIS

Always wash your hands as soon as you finish handling fresh chillis. The juice can cause severe irritation if brought in contact with delicate skin or your eyes.

CIDER VINEGAR

I have used this in the recipes because the malic acid which it contains helps digestion. It is also a traditional, though, as far as I know, unproven, aid to slimming.

MISO

This flavouring ingredient made from fermented soya beans is used in Miso Broth (page 177). You can buy miso from healthfood shops or stockists of oriental foods. It keeps indefinitely in the fridge.

NORI

These flat sheets of seaweed look like carbon paper. You should be able to get them at a healthfood shop. Nori is only used in Five-Star Salad (page 165) in this book, but it is a particularly valuable ingredient because it is very rich in iodine.

OLIVE OIL

This is the healthiest oil to use for cooking and the tastiest in salads.

QUARK

Quark is a soft white cheese, which is available in a low-fat version. Other low-fat smooth, soft white cheese could be used instead.

SESAME OIL

Just a few drops of sesame oil give a delicious nutty flavour to marinated tofu dishes and stir-fries.

SESAME CREAM

Also known as tahini, sesame cream is used in Hummus (page 182). It is available from healthfood shops and some supermarkets.

SOY SAUCE

Read the label to make sure that you are buying a properly fermented soy sauce which does not contain caramel or other additives and colourings. Tamari or Shoyu from the healthfood shop are excellent.

SPROUTED SEEDS

You can buy these at healthfood shops, or sprout them yourself at home. To do this, put 50 g/2 oz whole green lentils, mung beans or chickpeas into a sieve and place under cold running water for a few minutes. Rinse them under the tap twice a day. They will begin to sprout and should be ready in 3 days.

TARTEX

This is a vegetarian savoury pâté which is available from healthfood shops.

TOFU

Two types are available: silken tofu and firm tofu. The silken tofu is soft and suitable for making into dips and puddings; the firm tofu can be sliced and is best for savoury dishes. Firm tofu can be bought in flavoured varieties; try marinated and smoked tofu as well as plain. This is a useful ingredient because it is nutritious, yet low in calories. This book contains a number of recipes based on it.

SALADS

Choose vegetables that you like, preferably ones which need the minimum of preparation, and that are as fresh as possible. Ready-washed salads from supermarkets save time – just swish them through fresh water before using. Some ideas for quickly prepared salads are:

- crisp lettuce leaves or sliced tomatoes with sliced purple onions
- sliced cucumber with chopped herbs
- ready-washed watercress and chopped radishes
- chicory spears
- quartered little gem lettuce hearts
- sliced fennel and red pepper
- coarsely grated carrot with chopped parsley
- sliced tomato and salad cress
- chopped celery and sliced cucumber
- chopped cauliflower with tomato
- shredded red and white cabbage
- grated courgette, with lime juice
- beansprouts and watercress
- beansprouts, sliced raw mushrooms and soy sauce

It's surprising how quickly you can get used to less oily dressings. Fresh lemon or lime juice, with sea salt and freshly ground black pepper, makes a good dressing. Or you could try rice vinegar and balsamic vinegar. These are mellow and make excellent dressings on their own without any oil. If you are following the food-combining diet, do not use lemon juice or vinegar in a salad to be eaten with a carbohydrate dish. Just use oil, herbs or a little soured cream.

COLESLAW Ⓕⱽ, Ⓟ, Ⓥ

Serves 2, Calories per serving: 170

This salad keeps well in the fridge overnight in a covered container.

25 g/1 oz raisins or sultanas
350 g/12 oz white or red cabbage, finely shredded
100 g/4 oz carrots, scraped and coarsely grated
1 stick of celery, chopped

For the dressing

1 tablespoon Dijon mustard
1 tablespoon olive oil
1 tablespoon lemon juice
½ teaspoon caster sugar or honey
salt and freshly ground black pepper

Cover the raisins or sultanas with boiling water and leave them for a few minutes to plump. Put the cabbage, carrot and celery into a bowl. Make the dressing by mixing together the mustard, oil, lemon juice and sugar or honey. Then pour this over the cabbage mixture. Drain the raisins or sultanas and add these to the mixture; season with salt and freshly ground black pepper.

VARIATIONS

NUTTY COLESLAW Ⓟ, Ⓥ
Add 25 g/1 oz chopped hazelnuts to the mixture just before serving. This version serves two people at 230 Calories per serving.

CHEESY COLESLAW Ⓟ

Add 25 g/1 oz finely diced Cheddar cheese to the mixture just before serving. This version serves two people at 230 Calories per serving.

CREAMY COLESLAW Ⓟ

Make as above, but leave out the oil and vinegar. Add 1 × 100 g/4 oz carton of plain unsweetened yogurt and mix well. This version gives 130 Calories per serving.

GREEK SALAD Ⓟ

Serves 2, Calories per serving: 230

175 g/6 oz Feta cheese, cut into cubes
12 black olives
1 large beefsteak tomato, diced
½ large cucumber, peeled and diced
1 purple onion, skinned and sliced
juice of ½ lemon
freshly ground black pepper

Put the cheese into a bowl with the olives, tomato, cucumber and onion. Add the lemon juice and mix gently. Season with freshly ground black pepper.

FENNEL, RED PEPPER AND CARROT SALAD Ⓕⓥ, Ⓗⓣ, Ⓟ

Serves 4, Calories per serving: 40

Fennel is a useful low-Calorie vegetable with a refreshing aniseed flavour.

2 fennel bulbs, washed and thinly sliced
1 red pepper, de-seeded and cut into thin strips

225 g/8 oz carrots, coarsely grated
8 black olives
juice of 1 lemon
salt and freshly ground black pepper

Put the fennel into a bowl with the red pepper, grated
carrots, olives, lemon juice and some salt and pepper to
taste.

WATERCRESS AND TOMATO SALAD (FV), (HT), (P)

Serves 2, Calories per serving: 25

a packet or bunch of watercress
4 tomatoes, sliced
a squeeze of lemon juice
salt and freshly ground black pepper

Remove any tough stems and wash the watercress
thoroughly, then mix with the tomatoes and add the
lemon juice and some salt and pepper to taste.

VARIATION

WATERCRESS AND ORANGE SALAD (FV), (HT), (P), (V)

Use 2 large oranges, peeled and sliced, instead of the
tomatoes. This version gives 55 Calories per serving.

RAW SPINACH SALAD (FV), (HT), (P), (V)

Serves 2, Calories per serving: 100

225 g/8 oz fresh tender spinach leaves
2 tomatoes, skinned and chopped
100 g/4 oz tender button mushrooms, washed and
sliced
1 garlic clove, peeled and crushed
1 tablespoon olive oil
juice of ½ lemon
salt and freshly ground black pepper

Wash the spinach leaves carefully, then shred them finely
and put them into a bowl with the tomatoes, mushrooms,
garlic, oil and lemon. Add salt and pepper to taste and
mix well.

CUCUMBER, RASPBERRY AND ROSE PETAL SALAD (FV), (HT), (P), (V)

Serves 4, Calories per serving: 25

1 cucumber, peeled and sliced
100 g/4 oz raspberries
a handful of pink rose petals, shredded
1 tablespoon raspberry, cider or wine vinegar
1 teaspoon honey
salt and freshly ground black pepper

Put the cucumber into a bowl with the raspberries and
rose petals. Mix the vinegar with the honey and add to the
bowl. Season with salt and pepper. Serve immediately.

HERBS AND FLOWERS SALAD (FV), (HT), (P), (V)

Serves 1–2, Calories if serving 1: 30

1 packet of mixed continental leaves, or a selection
of different leaves (ordinary lettuce, frisée,
radicchio, red lettuce, batavia, etc), torn into
pieces
a few colourful edible flowers as available (e.g.
nasturtiums, marigolds, chive flowers, flowering
thyme or borage)
sprigs of fresh herbs as available, several types if
possible (e.g. marjoram, thyme, tarragon, chives
and a sage leaf)
1 tablespoon balsamic vinegar or 1 tablespoon wine
vinegar, sweetened with ½ teaspoon sugar or
honey

Put all the ingredients into a bowl and mix together
gently.

CABBAGE, APPLE AND SAGE SALAD (FV), (HT), (P), (V)

Serves 2, Calories per serving: 90

225 g/8 oz white cabbage
2 mellow eating apples
2 sage leaves
1 teaspoon honey
2 tablespoons cider vinegar

Shred the cabbage; peel and slice or chop the apples, and
chop the sage. Put these ingredients into a bowl or arrange
them on 2 plates. Mix together the honey and cider
vinegar and pour this dressing over the salad.

LETTUCE AND NASTURTIUM FLOWER SALAD Ⓕⓥ, Ⓗⓣ, Ⓟ, Ⓥ

Serves 2, Calories per serving: 30

1 lettuce (the ordinary type is fine)
a few curly endive leaves, if available
a few tender nasturtium leaves, if available
8 capers (optional)
1 teaspoon honey
1 tablespoon cider vinegar
salt and freshly ground black pepper
8 nasturtium flowers

Tear the lettuce and endive into pieces and put them into a bowl. Shred the nasturtium leaves and add them to the salad, together with the capers if using. Just before serving, mix together the honey, cider vinegar, salt and pepper and pour over the salad. Mix well, then decorate with the nasturtium flowers.

SPICED RICE WITH MARIGOLD PETALS Ⓒ, Ⓗⓣ, Ⓥ

Serves 4 as a main course
Calories per serving: 220

This can be served hot, to accompany a vegetable dish or salad; or it can be served cold, as a substantial salad in itself.

225 g/8 oz brown rice
½ teaspoon ground turmeric
½ teaspoon cumin seeds
½ teaspoon fennel seeds
6 black peppercorns
½ teaspoon salt

164

1 small green pepper, chopped
petals from 4–6 marigolds

Put the rice into a saucepan with the turmeric, cumin seeds, fennel seeds, black peppercorns, 600 ml/1 pint water and the salt. Bring to the boil, then cover and leave to cook very gently for 45 minutes. Check the seasoning, then add the chopped green pepper and the petals from the marigolds. Fork these ingredients through, then check the seasoning again. Serve at once. If you are planning to eat this cold, add the marigold petals later, just before serving.

FIVE-STAR SALAD (FV), (HT), (P), (V)

Serves 2, Calories per serving: 150

This salad contains five ingredients which are helpful for slimming.

2 raw beetroots
12 dandelion leaves
1 heart of celery
150 g/6 oz sprouted seeds (home-grown or bought)
1 tablespoon cider vinegar
1 teaspoon honey
1 teaspoon fennel seeds or 1 sheet of nori

Peel and coarsely grate the beetroot, wash and shred the dandelion leaves, and chop the celery. Put these ingredients into a bowl with the sprouted seeds, and mix in the cider vinegar and honey, and the fennel seeds if using. If you are using the nori, hold a sheet over a gas flame or electric burner for a few seconds, moving it about so that it becomes crisp all over, then crumble it into the salad. Serve immediately.

MAIN-COURSE SALAD (FV), (HT), (P), (V)

Serves 1–2
Calories without dressing if serving 1: 50
Calories with dressing if serving 1: 190

This salad can consist of any raw vegetables you like, so it can be different every time you make it.

a leaf vegetable (e.g. lettuce and/or watercress, lamb's lettuce or any other green salad, or crisp cabbage such as Primo)
a root vegetable (e.g. grated carrot and/or grated raw beetroot)
any other interesting vegetables as available (e.g. sliced onions, tomatoes, cucumber, celery, thinly sliced leeks, cauliflower florets, beansprouts, sliced red pepper, etc)
chopped fresh herbs as available

For the dressing

1–2 tablespoons olive oil
1–2 tablespoons rice vinegar
salt and freshly ground black pepper

Chop or tear the leaf vegetables and put them into a bowl or on a plate. Add the grated carrot and/or beetroot and any of the other vegetables and fresh herbs you are using, suitably chopped or sliced. Make a light dressing by mixing together the oil and vinegar. Add some salt and pepper, and pour over the salad.

SANDWICHES AND BAPS
Sandwiches

Use 2 slices of wholewheat or granary bread cut from a
large loaf and unbuttered as a basis for any of the following
fillings.

CHEESE AND TOMATO
Calories: 230

25 g/1 oz Edam cheese, sliced
1 tomato, sliced
salt and freshly ground black pepper

EGG MAYONNAISE
Calories: 250

1 hardboiled egg, finely chopped
2 tablespoons low-fat fromage frais
salt and freshly ground black pepper

FOOD-COMBINERS' EGG SANDWICHES ©
Calories: 330

2 hardboiled egg yolks, mashed with
2 tablespoons single cream
watercress
salt and freshly ground black pepper

EGG MAYONNAISE AND CRESS

Calories: 250

1 hardboiled egg, finely chopped
2 tablespoons low-fat fromage frais
cress
salt and freshly ground black pepper

QUARK AND TOMATO

Calories: 180

40 g/1½ oz quark
1 tomato, sliced
salt and freshly ground black pepper

QUARK AND PINEAPPLE

Calories: 200

40 g/1½ oz quark
1 canned-in-juice pineapple ring, drained and
chopped

QUARK AND GINGER

Calories: 210

40 g/1½ oz quark
1 knob or stem of crystallised ginger, chopped

QUARK AND CUCUMBER

Calories: 180

40 g/1½ oz quark
5 cm/2 in cucumber, sliced
salt and freshly ground black pepper

QUARK AND CRESS

Calories: 180

40 g/1½ oz quark
cress
salt and freshly ground black pepper

TARTEX AND CRESS ⓥ

Calories: 210

25 g/1 oz Tartex Swiss vegetable pâté
cress

TARTEX AND CUCUMBER ⓥ

Calories: 210

25 g/1 oz Tartex Swiss vegetable pâté
5 cm/2 in cucumber, sliced

MARMITE AND CUCUMBER ⓒ, ⓥ

Calories: 210

7 g/¼ oz soft butter
Marmite
5 cm/2 in cucumber, sliced

TOMATO AND ONION ⓒ, ⓥ

Calories: 220

7 g/¼ oz soft butter
1 large tomato
a few slices of onion
salt and freshly ground black pepper

CREAMY CARROT ⓒ

Calories: 220

1–2 carrots, grated
2 tablespoons soured cream
chopped herbs
salt and freshly ground black pepper

Mix the carrot and soured cream together, then add the herbs and seasoning.

MUSHROOM PÂTÉ ⓒ, ⓥ

Calories: 210

Use half the quantity given in the Mushroom Pâté recipe on page 181.

SALAD ⓒ, ⓥ

Calories: 170

lettuce
1 tomato, sliced
a little grated carrot
a few cucumber slices

Baps

CHEESE AND PICKLE BAP

Serves 1, Calories: 300

1 bap
40 g/1½ oz Cheddar cheese, sliced
1 tablespoon pickle

Halve the bap, fill with the slices of cheese, spread with pickle and press the 2 halves together.

VARIATIONS

CHEESE AND TOMATO BAP

Omit the pickle and use 1 small tomato, sliced, instead. This version has 300 Calories.

CHEESE AND ONION BAP

Instead of the pickle use 1 small onion, sliced. This version also gives 300 Calories.

SOUPS

ROOT VEGETABLE SOUP Ⓕⓥ, Ⓗⓣ, Ⓟ, Ⓥ

Serves 4
Calories per serving without cream: 40
Calories with cream: 70

350 g/12 oz carrots, peeled and diced
225 g/8 oz swede, peeled and diced
1 large garlic clove, peeled
1 tablespoon lemon juice
4 tablespoons single cream (optional)
salt and freshly ground black pepper

Put the carrots, swede and garlic into a large saucepan with 1 litre/1¾ pints water and simmer for 15–20 minutes, or until the vegetables are tender. Liquidise the soup, then return to the saucepan, and add the lemon juice, and cream if using. Season with salt and pepper to taste.

VARIATION

CHILLED ROOT VEGETABLE SOUP WITH LIME Ⓕⓥ, Ⓗⓣ, Ⓟ, Ⓥ

Make the soup as described but omit the lemon juice. Pare off some thin strips of rind from 1 lime – a zester is excellent for doing this – and squeeze the juice. Add some of the juice to the soup, to give a pleasantly sharp flavour. Chill, and serve with a few strips of peel in each bowl. The Calories are the same.

CURRIED TOMATO AND APPLE SOUP (FV), (HT), (P), (V)

Serves 4
Calories per serving without cream: 90
Calories per serving with cream: 120

1 onion, peeled and chopped
1 tablespoon olive oil
1 eating apple, peeled and chopped
2 carrots, peeled and diced
1 garlic clove, peeled and crushed
2 teaspoons curry powder
1 × 400 g/14 oz can tomatoes
juice of 1 orange
salt and freshly ground black pepper
4 tablespoons single cream (optional)

Fry the onion in the oil for 5 minutes, then add the apple, carrots, garlic and curry powder, and fry for a further 5 minutes. Add the tomatoes and 600 ml/1 pint water, cover and simmer for 15 minutes, or until the vegetables are tender. Liquidise the soup very thoroughly, then add the orange juice, salt and pepper to taste, and the cream if using.

HEARTY VEGETABLE SOUP Ⓕⓥ, Ⓗⓣ, Ⓝ, Ⓥ

Serves 4, Calories per serving: 100

450 g/1 lb aubergines, diced
salt and freshly ground black pepper
1 tablespoon olive oil
1 onion, peeled and chopped
450 g/1 lb courgettes, diced
225 g/8 oz carrots, peeled and sliced
100 g/4 oz celery, diced
1 green pepper, de-seeded and diced
1 red pepper, de-seeded and diced

Put the aubergine into a colander, sprinkle with salt, put
a plate and a weight on top, and leave for 20 minutes.
Then rinse under the cold tap and squeeze as dry as you
can. Heat the oil in a large saucepan and fry the onion for
5 minutes, then add the aubergines, courgettes, carrots,
celery, and the green and red peppers. Fry for 5 minutes
before adding 300 ml/10 fl oz water. Cover and cook
gently for about 30 minutes, or until all the vegetables are
tender. Season with salt and freshly ground black pepper.

LENTIL SOUP Ⓗⓣ, Ⓥ

Serves 4, Calories per serving: 140

100 g/4 oz green lentils
1 carrot, peeled and cut into chunks
2 onions, peeled and chopped
1 tablespoon olive oil
salt and freshly ground black pepper

Put the lentils into a saucepan with 1.5 litres/2½ pints

174

water, the carrot and half the onion. Bring to the boil, then simmer for 45–50 minutes, until the lentils are tender. Heat the oil in another saucepan and fry the rest of the onion for 10 minutes, until soft and lightly browned. Add the onion to the lentil mixture, then liquidise the soup. Reheat and season with salt and pepper.

POTATO AND ONION SOUP Ⓒ, ⒻⓋ, ⒽⓉ, Ⓥ

Serves 4
Calories per serving without cream: 150
Calories per serving with cream: 180

450 g/1 lb potatoes, peeled and diced
2 onions, peeled and chopped
15 g/½ oz butter
4 tablespoons single cream (optional)
salt and freshly ground black pepper
freshly grated nutmeg

Put the potatoes and half the onion into a large saucepan with 1 litre/1¾ pints water and simmer for 15–20 minutes, or until the vegetables are cooked. Meanwhile, melt the butter in another saucepan and gently fry the remaining onion for about 10 minutes until tender. Liquidise the soup and add the cream if using. Then add the fried onion, and season with salt, pepper and nutmeg to taste.

CARROT SOUP Ⓒ, Ⓕⓥ, Ⓗⓣ, Ⓥ

Serves 4, Calories per serving: 120

15 g/½ oz butter
1 onion, finely chopped
450 g/1 lb carrots, peeled and diced
750 g/1½ lb potatoes, peeled and diced
1–2 teaspoons sugar
salt and freshly ground black pepper
freshly grated nutmeg

Melt the butter in a large saucepan. Put in the onion, carrots and potatoes, cover and cook gently, without browning, for 10 minutes. Then add 1 litre/1¾ pints water, cover, and simmer for about 20 minutes, or until the vegetables are tender. Liquidise, then add sugar to taste and season with salt, pepper and nutmeg.

WATERCRESS SOUP Ⓒ, Ⓕⓥ, Ⓗⓣ, Ⓥ

Serves 4
Calories per serving without cream: 110
Calories per serving with cream: 140

450 g/1 lb potatoes, peeled and diced
1 onion, peeled and chopped
1 bunch of watercress, washed
4 tablespoons single cream (optional)
salt and freshly ground black pepper

Put the potatoes and onion into a large saucepan with 1 litre/1¾ pints water and the watercress stalks (reserve the leaves for later). Simmer for 15–20 minutes, or until the vegetables are tender. Liquidise the soup with the reserved leaves, and add the cream if using. Season with salt and pepper to taste.

MISO BROTH Ⓗ, Ⓝ, Ⓥ

Serves 4, Calories per serving: 25

1 teaspoon vegetarian stock powder
1 tablespoon white or red miso
4 spring onions, washed and sliced
4 radishes, sliced
a few sprigs of mustard and cress, to serve

Put 1.2 litres/2 pints water and the stock powder into a saucepan and bring to the boil. Put the miso into a bowl, soften with a little of the boiling stock, then add to the rest of the stock in the pan. Heat, but do not boil. Divide the spring onions and radishes between 4 bowls, pour in the miso mixture and sprinkle with a few sprigs of mustard and cress. Serve immediately.

CHILLED CUCUMBER AND YOGURT SOUP Ⓕⓥ, Ⓗ, Ⓟ

Serves 4, Calories per serving: 65

1 cucumber, peeled and roughly chopped
1 garlic clove, peeled and crushed
1 × 225 g/8 oz carton Greek yogurt
salt and freshly ground black pepper
chopped chives, to serve

Liquidise the cucumber with the garlic and yogurt, and season with salt and pepper. Chill the soup thoroughly, then serve in individual bowls, with a sprinkling of chopped chives on top.

DIPS, SAUCES AND STARTERS
Dips

Keep one or two of these low-Calorie dips made up and in the fridge, together with washed and prepared vegetables – carrot, celery and cucumber sticks, cauliflower florets, spring onions – to make it easy (or easier) to keep to your diet when you want something to munch.

RICE VINEGAR (HT), (P), (V)

No Calories

This is good just as it is. Pour it into a small bowl straight from the bottle.

HERB VINEGARS (HT), (P), (V)

No calories

For a change, try flavouring the rice vinegar by adding chopped or dried herbs – this is a good way of getting to know the flavours of different herbs. Fresh or dried dill is particularly good; also tarragon, lovage and mint. Crushed garlic and grated fresh ginger can also be added, as can coarsely crushed black peppercorns or coriander seeds (use a pestle and mortar or the flat end of a rolling pin).

BALSAMIC VINEGAR (HT), (P), (V)

No Calories

Like rice vinegar, delicious as it is, or with the additions suggested.

SOY SAUCE (HT), (N), (V)

Calories per tablespoon: 13

This is also good on its own, or with grated fresh ginger or crushed garlic added.

MUSTARD DIP (HT), (P), (V)

Calories: 40

Mix together 1 tablespoon Dijon or Meaux mustard, 1 tablespoon soy sauce and 1 tablespoon rice vinegar or balsamic vinegar. Crushed garlic and/or grated fresh ginger can be added.

YOGURT AND HERBS (HT), (P)

Calories: 20

Mix together 2 tablespoons plain unsweetened yogurt with some chopped fresh herbs (mint and chives are good) and season with salt and freshly ground black pepper.

CURRIED DIP (HT), (P)

Calories: 30

Add ½–1 teaspoon curry paste or powder to 2 tablespoons plain unsweetened yogurt. Mix well, and season with salt and freshly ground black pepper.

LOW-CALORIE SALAD CREAM (HT)

Calories per tablespoon: around 20

1–2 tablespoons of your favourite low-Calorie salad cream.

CITRUS DIP (HT), (P), (V)

No Calories

Mix the grated rind of a lemon or lime in a small bowl with some of the juice. Add a few chopped herbs, and some crushed black peppercorns or coriander seeds as well if you like.

TOMATO COULIS (FV), (HT), (P), (V)

Serves 4, Calories per serving: 70

This is a very useful low-Calorie sauce which goes with many dishes. It freezes well, so is worth making up in bulk and freezing in small portions to save time.

1 tablespoon olive oil
1 onion, peeled and chopped
450 g/1 lb tomatoes, skinned, or 425 g/15 oz can
salt and freshly ground black pepper

Heat the oil in a saucepan and fry the onion gently for about 10 minutes, until softened. Chop the tomatoes and add to the onion. Cook for 20–30 minutes, with a lid on the pan, until the mixture is purée-like. Season with salt and freshly ground black pepper.

Note: If you are following the Food-Combining method of slimming, remember this sauce does not combine with carbohydrates because of the cooked tomato. However, you can adapt it by frying the onion until soft, cooling, and then adding the fresh, skinned, chopped tomatoes, and some seasoning, to make a cold sauce. Either the hot or the cold sauce can be flavoured with a garlic clove, fried with the onion, or a tablespoonful of chopped basil, added just before serving.

MUSHROOM PÂTÉ (FV), (HT), (N), (V)

Serves 1, Calories: 130

**225 g/8 oz white button mushrooms
15 g/½ oz butter
salt and freshly ground black pepper and freshly
grated nutmeg**

Wash the mushrooms, then chop them finely — a food
processor is best for this. Fry the mushrooms in the butter
for about 10 minutes, or until any liquid from the
mushrooms has disappeared and the mushrooms are
tender. Season with salt, pepper and nutmeg; spoon the
mixture into a small bowl or ramekin; cool, then chill.

TSATSIKI (FV), (HT), (P)

Serves 1, Calories: 70

**½ cucumber
salt and freshly ground black pepper
1 × 100 g/4 oz carton plain low-fat yogurt
lettuce leaves, to serve
a little chopped fresh mint if available**

Peel and dice the cucumber. Put it into a sieve or colander
and sprinkle with salt. Cover with a plate, put a weight on
top and leave to drain for at least 30 minutes. Then
squeeze out any excess moisture and put the cucumber
into a bowl. Mix in the yogurt and season as necessary.
Spoon the mixture on top of crisp lettuce leaves and top
with a little chopped mint.

HUMMUS (HT), (V)

Serves 2–4
Calories if serving 2: 240
Calories if serving 4: 120

1 × 400 g/14 oz can chickpeas
1 garlic clove, peeled and crushed
1 teaspoon sesame cream
juice of 1 lemon
2 tablespoons olive oil
salt and freshly ground black pepper

Drain the chickpeas, reserving the liquid. Mash the chickpeas thoroughly, or whizz them in a food processor, adding a little of the liquid if necessary. Add the garlic, sesame cream, lemon juice and oil, and mix thoroughly or whizz again. Add just enough of the reserved liquid to give a creamy consistency. Season with salt and freshly ground black pepper. Serve with some strips of warmed pitta bread and/or some raw vegetables such as small florets of cauliflower, sticks of scraped carrot, celery sticks, strips of red or green pepper, spring onions, sticks of cucumber and radishes.

Starters

GLOBE ARTICHOKES ⒡ⓥ, ⒣ⓣ, Ⓝ, ⓥ

Serves 4, Calories per serving: 80

4 globe artichokes
salt and freshly ground black pepper
25 g/1 oz butter, melted

Cut the stems off the artichokes and trim the points off the leaves with scissors. Put the artichokes in a saucepan with enough water to cover, and boil for 45 minutes, or until you can pull one of the leaves off easily. Drain well. Then, when the artichokes are cool enough to handle, prise each one open and pull out the central cluster of tiny leaves. With a teaspoon, scrape out and discard the fibrous 'choke' which lies under the tiny leaves. Serve the artichokes with the melted butter for dipping.

MARINATED MELON ⒣ⓣ, ⓥ

Serves 1, Calories: 150

1 thick slice honeydew melon
3 tablespoons Midori (melon liqueur), or other
liqueur such as Chartreuse or Kirsch
a few thin slices of orange, 2–3 halved black
grapes, cherries, raspberries or strawberries, to
decorate

Cut the skin off the melon, then slice the flesh into long thin pieces or dice. Lay the pieces on a plate and sprinkle evenly with the liqueur. Decorate with some thinly sliced orange, or grapes, cherries and raspberries or strawberries.

GARLIC MUSHROOMS (FV), (HT), (N), (V)

Serves 4, Calories per serving: 45

1 tablespoon olive oil
450 g/1 lb small button mushrooms, wiped and
sliced
2 garlic cloves, peeled and crushed
salt and freshly ground black pepper

Heat the oil in a saucepan, then add the mushrooms and
garlic. Cook for about 5 minutes, until the mushrooms
are tender. If they produce some liquid, continue to cook
over a high heat until all the liquid has boiled away. This
might take another 5 minutes or so. Season with salt and
pepper and serve immediately.

ASPARAGUS WITH LEMON VINAIGRETTE (FV), (HT), (P), (V)

Serves 4, Calories per serving: 60

24 fat asparagus spears
1 tablespoon olive oil
juice of ½ lemon
salt and freshly ground black pepper

Trim off the tough ends and wash the asparagus thoroughly to dislodge any grit. Pour 1 cm/½ in water into a
large frying pan or wide saucepan, then put the asparagus
into the water, cover with a plate or lid, and boil for 5–10
minutes, or until just tender. (The exact timing will
depend on how thick the stems are.) Drain well. Mix
together the oil and lemon juice and sprinkle over the
asparagus. Season with salt and pepper. Serve hot or cold.

MINTY GRAPEFRUIT (FV), (HT), (P), (V)

Serves 1, Calories: 140

1 grapefruit
1 large orange
1 tablespoon chopped mint
½–1 teaspoon caster sugar or honey (optional)
crisp lettuce leaves to serve (optional)
a few sprigs of mint (optional)

First peel the grapefruit and orange using a sawing motion and cutting round and round as if you were peeling an apple. Then cut the segments out from between the membranes and put them into a bowl. Add the mint, and sugar or honey to taste. Serve in a bowl or over lettuce leaves, garnished with a few sprigs of fresh mint if you wish.

VEGETABLE DISHES

Serving a good portion of low-Calorie vegetables with a main course is a very good way of filling you up whilst keeping the Calories down.

Choose any vegetables you really like, either fresh or frozen, except the very starchy ones such as potatoes, beetroot, parsnip, beans or sweetcorn. And reduce the time you spend in the kitchen by choosing vegetables which are easy to prepare, or buying them ready-prepared from the supermarket. Here are a few tips on cooking and serving vegetables:

- Cut the vegetables into even-sized pieces and cook them for the minimum length of time.
- It's best to cook them either in a steamer on top of a saucepan, or in one of those flower-like steamers you can buy quite cheaply.
- Another method is to bring a bare 1 cm/½ in water to the boil in a saucepan, then add the vegetables, cooking for a few minutes, covered, until just tender, and drain.
- Serve the vegetables sprinkled with chopped fresh herbs, a squeeze of fresh lemon juice (food-combiners see page 158) and perhaps some of the grated rind, some crunchy sea salt (Tidman's, from the healthfood shop), some coarsely ground or crushed black peppercorns or coriander seeds, or some soy sauce or rice vinegar.

ANISEED CARROTS (FV), (HT), (P), (V)

Serves 3–4, Calories per serving: 50

750 g/1½ lb carrots
2 tablespoons lemon juice
1 tablespoon aniseed
salt and freshly ground black pepper

Peel or scrape the carrots and cut into slices or matchsticks. Bring 1 cm/½ in water to the boil and add the carrots. Then cover and cook for 10–15 minutes, until the carrots are just tender. Drain and add the lemon juice, aniseed and salt and pepper to taste.

BRAISED MARROW (FV), (HT), (N), (V)

Serves 2–4
Calories per serving for 4: 50
Calories per serving for 2: 100

1 tender marrow (about 750 g/1½ lb)
15 g/½ oz butter
salt and freshly ground black pepper
1–2 tablespoons chopped fresh herbs

Peel and dice the marrow. If the marrow is tender, there will be no need to remove the seeds. Melt the butter in a large saucepan and add the marrow. Stir gently, then cover and leave to cook over a moderate heat for about 10 minutes, or until the marrow is tender, golden and almost translucent. Season with salt and pepper and sprinkle with the fresh herbs.

AUBERGINE WITH SOY AND GINGER (FV), (HT), (N), (V)

Serves 2–4
Calories per serving for 2 people: 60
Calories per serving for 4 people: 30

2 medium aubergines
4 tablespoons soy sauce
2 teaspoons grated fresh ginger
2 garlic cloves, peeled and crushed

Cut the aubergines into circles or strips, then cook them in a little boiling water for 3–5 minutes, until tender. Drain well, then spread the pieces out in a shallow dish. Mix together the soy sauce, ginger and garlic, and pour this mixture over the aubergine slices. Leave the aubergine to marinate for 15 minutes, or longer if there is time, turning the slices or strips so that they all soak up the marinade. Serve warm.

MARINATED TOFU AND VEGETABLE KEBABS (HT), (V)

Serves 2–4
Calories per serving for 2 people: 160
Calories per serving for 4 people: 80

Serve with plain boiled rice, an extra 200 Calories per 50 g/2 oz (dry weight).

1 × 225 g/8 oz packet marinated tofu, drained
2 medium tomatoes
½ medium green pepper, de-seeded
½ small onion, peeled
12 very small button mushrooms or 6 larger ones
4 tablespoons soy sauce
2 teaspoons sesame oil

Cut the tofu into 16 chunks. Then cut each tomato into 6 segments, the green pepper into 12 squarish pieces, and the onion into chunky slices; if the mushrooms are large, cut each in half. Thread these ingredients on to 4 skewers: start with a cube of tofu, then some green pepper, a piece of tomato, mushroom, and a strip of onion. Repeat, ending with a cube of tofu, and using 4 cubes of tofu per skewer. Put the kebabs in a shallow heatproof dish and sprinkle the soy sauce and sesame oil on top. Grill for about 7 minutes, until the ingredients are all heated through. Serve with plain boiled rice or a mixture of stir-fried vegetables (page 189).

SPICED VEGETABLES Ⓕⓥ, Ⓗⓣ, Ⓝ, Ⓥ

Serves 4, Calories per serving: 160

2 tablespoons olive oil
1 teaspoon mustard seeds
2 teaspoons turmeric
14 curry leaves, fresh or dried, or ½ teaspoon
curry powder
4 garlic cloves, peeled and crushed
4 cm/1½ in fresh ginger, peeled and grated
¼ teaspoon hot chilli powder
1 medium cauliflower, broken into florets, to make
750 g/1½ lb
100 g/4 oz green beans, topped and tailed
225 g/8 oz carrots, scraped and sliced
about 8 outside leaves of the cauliflower, washed
and chopped
salt and freshly ground black pepper

Heat the oil in a large saucepan, then add the mustard
seeds, turmeric, curry leaves or powder, garlic, ginger
and chilli. Fry for 2 minutes without burning, then add
the cauliflower, beans, carrots, and cauliflower leaves.
Mix well and cook gently for 15–20 minutes, until the
vegetables are almost tender. Season with salt and pepper.

Stir-Fry Dishes

A stir-fry is really like a heated salad. It's a quick and
healthy way of cooking vegetables but you do need a large
pan or, preferably, a wok, to cook it.

189

• Choose your favourite vegetables, allowing about 350 g/12 oz vegetables per person.
• Cut the vegetables into fairly small pieces.
• Heat the oil before you begin, and put the vegetables which take longest to cook into the pan or wok first.
• Add any flavourings you fancy, such as crushed garlic, grated fresh ginger, a tablespoonful of soy sauce, a few drops of seasame oil, or chopped fresh herbs if available.
• Then add any extras you like, such as sunflower seeds, toasted under the grill (160 Calories per 25 g/1 oz), roasted peanuts (170 Calories per 25 g/1 oz), blanched and slivered almonds (170 Calories per 25 g/1 oz), or cubes or slices of tofu sprinkled with soy sauce (15 Calories per 25 g/1 oz).

STIR-FRIED BEANSPROUTS, CARROTS AND GREEN PEPPER (FV), (HT), (N), (V)

Serves 2, Calories per serving: 150

225 g/8 oz carrots, peeled
1 green pepper, de-seeded
1 tablespoon olive oil
225 g/8 oz beansprouts
2 tablespoons soy sauce
freshly ground black pepper

Slice the carrots and green pepper into thin matchsticks. Then heat the oil in a large saucepan or wok and add the carrots and pepper. Cook for 4 minutes, until they begin to soften, then add the beansprouts and stir-fry for 1–2 minutes, to heat through. Add the soy sauce and some black pepper, and serve at once.

VEGETABLE STIR-FRY WITH MARINATED TOFU Ⓗⓣ, Ⓟ, Ⓥ

Serves 4, Calories per serving: 160

450 g/1 lb firm tofu, drained
4 tablespoons soy sauce
1 teaspoon dark sesame oil
1 tablespoon olive oil
2 garlic cloves, peeled and crushed
2.5 cm/1 in ginger root, grated
350 g/12 oz broccoli, broken into florets, stems
sliced thinly
1 red pepper, de-seeded and sliced
450 g/1 lb courgettes, sliced
100 g/4 oz mangetout, topped and tailed
100 g/4 oz baby sweetcorn, sliced diagonally
a bunch of spring onions, trimmed and sliced

Dice the tofu and spread the pieces out on a plate. Mix together the soy sauce and sesame oil, and sprinkle this over the tofu, making sure all the pieces are coated. Leave for at least 1 hour – or even overnight – to allow the tofu to absorb the flavours, stirring occasionally. To make the stir-fry, heat the olive oil in a large saucepan or wok and fry the garlic and ginger for a few seconds. Now put in the broccoli and red pepper, and stir-fry for 2 minutes. Then add the rest of the vegetables, and the tofu, and stir for a further few minutes, until everything is heated through. Serve at once.

CITRUS-MARINATED TOFU WITH STIR-FRIED VEGETABLES (HT), (P), (V)

Serves 2, Calories per serving: 210

1 × 225 g/8 oz packet firm tofu, drained
2 garlic cloves, peeled and crushed
rind and juice of 1 lemon or lime
2 tablespoons chopped parsley
1 green chilli, de-seeded and finely chopped
2 tablespoons soy sauce
1 tablespoon olive oil
225 g/8 oz Chinese leaves or white cabbage,
shredded
100 g/4 oz carrots, cut into matchsticks
1 green pepper, de-seeded and cut into matchsticks
a bunch of spring onions, chopped

Cut the tofu into slices and put them in a shallow dish.
Mix together the garlic, lemon or lime juice and rind,
parsley, chilli and soy sauce. Pour this mixture over the
tofu, and leave to marinate for at least 30 minutes,
preferably for several hours. When you are ready to serve
the dish, heat the oil in a large saucepan or wok and add
the vegetables. Stir-fry for about 4 minutes, or until
heated through. Then add the tofu and any remaining
liquid from the marinade. Stir-fry for a further 2 minutes
or so, until heated through, and serve.

SWEET AND SOUR VEGETABLE STIR-FRY (HT), (V)

Serves 2, Calories per serving: 180

Serve with cooked brown rice,
an extra 100 Calories per 25 g/1 oz

1 tablespoon olive oil
1 green pepper, skinned with a potato peeler, de-
seeded and sliced
100 g/4 oz cabbage, shredded
225 g/8 oz beansprouts, washed
100 g/4 oz button mushrooms, sliced
225 g/8 oz can pineapple pieces
1 teaspoon cornflour
2 tablespoons soy sauce
salt and freshly ground black pepper

Heat the oil in a large saucepan or wok. Put in the green
pepper and cabbage and stir-fry for 2 minutes. Then add
the beansprouts, mushrooms and pineapple, and stir-fry
for a further 2–3 minutes, until heated through. Quickly
mix the cornflour with the soy sauce, and add this to the
mixture, stirring. Cook for a further 1–2 minutes, season
with salt and pepper, and serve.

Vegetable Bakes and Casseroles

PROVENÇAL STEW Ⓗ, Ⓟ, Ⓥ

Serves 4, Calories per serving: 290

1 tablespoon olive oil
1 large onion, peeled and sliced
1 garlic clove, peeled and crushed
1 red pepper, de-seeded and chopped
450 g/1 lb courgettes, sliced
1 aubergine, diced
450 g/1 lb tomatoes, skinned and chopped
225 g/8 oz button mushrooms, sliced (optional)
2 × 400 g/14 oz cans flageolet beans
salt and freshly ground black pepper
chopped parsley, to serve

Heat the oil in a large saucepan and add the onion. Fry gently for 5 minutes, then add the garlic, red pepper, courgettes and aubergine. Stir, then cover and cook gently for a further 10 minutes, stirring often to prevent sticking. Add the tomatoes, mushrooms if using, and flageolet beans, then simmer gently for 20–25 minutes, until all the vegetables are cooked. Season with salt and freshly ground black pepper. Sprinkle with chopped fresh parsley and serve.

VARIATION

FOOD-COMBINERS' PROVENÇAL STEW Ⓗ, Ⓟ, Ⓥ
The flageolet beans can be omitted if preferred.

AUBERGINE BAKE

Serves 4, Calories per serving: 210

2 × 750 g/1½ lb aubergines, cut into 1 cm/½ in
cubes
salt and freshly ground black pepper
3 tomatoes, chopped
2 garlic cloves, peeled and crushed
½ teaspoon oregano
1 tablespoon olive oil
100 g/4 oz fresh wholemeal breadcrumbs
50 g/2 oz Mozzarella cheese, grated
4 tablespoons grated Parmesan cheese

Sprinkle the aubergine with salt. Leave for 30 minutes,
then rinse under cold water and drain. Preheat the oven to
200°C/400°F/Gas Mark 6. Put the aubergine chunks into
a bowl with the tomatoes, garlic, oregano and olive oil,
and mix well. Spoon into a shallow casserole dish, and
sprinkle the breadcrumbs and grated cheese on top. Bake
for 45 minutes, or until the aubergine is very tender and
the topping golden brown.

VARIATIONS

VEGAN AUBERGINE BAKE (HT), (V)
If you don't eat dairy produce, just leave out the cheese.
This version gives 130 Calories per serving.

FOOD-COMBINERS' AUBERGINE BAKE (P)

Omit the breadcrumbs. This is a protein dish.

GRATIN OF VEGETABLES Ⓟ

Serves 4, Calories per serving: 260

You can vary the vegetables according to what is available, but, if you're following food-combining, don't use potatoes.

225 g/8 oz celery, sliced
225 g/8 oz parsnips, peeled and diced
225 g/8 oz carrots, peeled and diced
225 g/8 oz onions, peeled and sliced
225 g/8 oz leeks, cleaned and sliced
225 g/8 oz mushrooms, washed and sliced
175 g/6 oz Cheddar cheese, grated
salt and freshly ground black pepper

Cook all the vegetables except the mushrooms together in boiling water until they are just tender, then drain. Preheat the oven to 200°C/400°F/Gas Mark 6. Add half the grated cheese, and the mushrooms, to the vegetables, and some salt and pepper to taste. Spoon the mixture into a shallow ovenproof dish and sprinkle with the remaining cheese. Cook in the oven for about 30 minutes, or until golden brown and crisp on top.

RATATOUILLE Ⓕⓥ, Ⓗⓣ, Ⓟ, Ⓥ

Serves 4, Calories per serving: 100

This is good served with a baked potato, or boiled rice mixed with chopped fresh herbs.

2 medium aubergines (about 350 g/12 oz together)
4–6 courgettes (about 350 g/12 oz together)
salt and freshly ground black pepper
1 tablespoon olive oil
1 large onion, peeled and chopped
2 garlic cloves, peeled and crushed
2–3 green peppers, skinned with a potato peeler,
de-seeded and chopped
1 × 400 g/14 oz can tomatoes, liquidised
2 tablespoons tomato purée
½–1 teaspoon sugar

Cut the aubergines and courgettes into small dice, put them in a colander and sprinkle with salt. Cover with a plate, put a weight on top, and leave for 30 minutes. Then rinse, and drain well. Heat the oil in a large saucepan and fry the onion for 5 minutes, then add the garlic and green peppers, and the drained aubergines and courgettes. Stir, then fry, covered, for a further 5 minutes. Add the liquidised tomatoes and tomato purée, cover, and cook gently for 30 minutes. Add the sugar, and season with salt and pepper.

VEGETABLE GOULASH ⓕⓥ, ⓗⓣ, ⓥ

Serves 2
Calories per serving without cream: 230
Calories per serving with cream: 280

1 tablespoon olive oil
2 large onions, peeled and sliced
2 garlic cloves, peeled and crushed
1 tablespoon paprika
2 green peppers, skinned with a potato peeler, de-
seeded and chopped
225 g/8 oz leeks, washed, trimmed and sliced
225 g/8 oz carrots, peeled and sliced
450 g/1 lb tomatoes, skinned and chopped
2 tablespoons tomato purée
salt and freshly ground black pepper
4 tablespoons soured cream (optional)

Heat the oil in a large saucepan and add the onion. Fry gently for 5 minutes, then add the garlic, paprika, green peppers, leeks and carrots. Stir, then cover and cook gently for a further 10 minutes, stirring often to prevent sticking. Add the tomatoes and tomato purée, then simmer gently for 20–25 minutes, stirring occasionally, until all the vegetables are cooked. Season with salt and freshly ground black pepper. Serve with a tablespoonful of soured cream on each portion, if liked.

STUFFED AUBERGINE ⓟ

Serves 4, Calories per serving: 180

2 medium-sized aubergines, about 350 g/12 oz each
1 tablespoon olive oil
1 onion, peeled and chopped
1 garlic clove, crushed
225 g/8 oz button mushrooms
½ teaspoon thyme
25 g/1 oz flaked almonds
50 g/2 oz Cheddar cheese, grated
squeeze of lemon juice
salt and freshly ground black pepper

Remove the stalks from the aubergines. Place the aubergines in a baking tin and bake in a moderate oven for about 30 minutes, or until they feel tender when squeezed. Cool, then cut the aubergines in half across and scoop out the flesh, leaving the skins whole. Chop the scooped-out flesh and leave on one side. Preheat the oven to 200°C/400°F/Gas Mark 6. Heat the oil in a saucepan and fry the onion for 5 minutes, then add the garlic and mushrooms and fry for a further 5 minutes, or until any liquid which the mushrooms produce has boiled away. Add the thyme, scooped-out aubergine pulp, almonds, half the cheese, lemon juice and salt and pepper to taste. Spoon this mixture into the aubergine skins, sprinkle with the rest of the cheese, and bake for 20–30 minutes, or until golden brown.

VEGAN VARIATION ⓗⓣ, ⓟ, ⓥ

Use 25g/1 oz ground almonds instead of the grated cheese. This version gives 160 Calories per serving.

QUICK VEGETABLE HOTPOT Ⓒ, ⒻⓋ, ⒽⓉ, Ⓥ

Serves 2, Calories per serving: 290

15 g/½ oz butter or margarine
2 leeks, washed, trimmed and sliced
350 g/12 oz potatoes, peeled and cut into even-
sized pieces
350 g/12 oz carrots, peeled and sliced
salt and freshly ground black pepper
chopped parsley, to serve

Melt the butter or margarine in a saucepan, then add the
leeks and fry gently for 5 minutes, without browning.
Add the potatoes, stir, then add 250 ml/8 fl oz water.
Cover and cook gently for about 20 minutes, or until the
potatoes are tender and the water has been absorbed.
Season with salt and pepper, sprinkle with chopped
parsley, and serve.

POTATO DISHES

BAKED POTATO WITH SOURED CREAM AND ASPARAGUS Ⓒ, ⒽⓉ

Serves 1, Calories: 290

1 medium potato (about 275 g/10 oz)
1 tablespoon soured cream
2 large asparagus spears
salt and freshly ground black pepper

Scrub the potato, then prick it in several places to allow the steam to escape. Bake at 230°C/450°F/Gas Mark 8 for about 1½ hours, or until the skin is crisp and the inside is tender when pierced with a sharp knife. Meanwhile, remove the tough stalk ends from the asparagus and cook it in 1 cm/½ in boiling water for 5–7 minutes, until just tender. Drain and cut into 2.5 cm/1 in lengths. To serve, place the potato on a plate, split it into 2 halves, spoon the soured cream into the centre, top with the asparagus and season with salt and pepper.

VARIATION

SWEETCORN POTATO Ⓒ, ⒣⒯, Ⓥ

Omit the soured cream and asparagus. Instead, heat up 50 g/2 oz canned sweetcorn and spoon into the centre of the potato. This version gives 300 Calories.

SLIMMERS' CHIPS Ⓒ, ⒣⒯, Ⓥ

Serves 1, Calories: 350

A very satisfying crunchy slimmers' version of chips. Much more to eat for a fraction of the Calories.

1 large potato (about 350 g/12 oz)
1 teaspoon sunflower oil

Preheat the oven to 200°C/400°F/Gas Mark 6. Peel the potato and cut into chunky chips. Sprinkle the oil over the chips, then turn them with your hands to make sure they are all lightly coated. Place the chips in a single layer on a baking tray and bake for about 45 minutes, or until crisp and golden brown, turning them over after about 35 minutes.

201

CHEESY BAKED POTATO

Serves 1, Calories: 300

1 × 225 g/8 oz potato
2 tablespoons skimmed milk
25 g/1 oz Edam cheese, grated
salt and freshly ground black pepper
1 tomato, sliced

Scrub the potato, then prick it in several places to allow the steam to escape. Bake at 230°C/450°F/Gas Mark 8 for about 1½ hours, or until the skin is crisp and the inside is tender when pierced with a sharp knife. Holding the potato in a cloth, cut it in half horizontally, then scoop the potato out of the skins without damaging them. Mash the potato with the skimmed milk and half the grated cheese. Season with salt and pepper, then spoon the mixture back into the skins. Sprinkle with the rest of the cheese and top with the tomato slices. Return to the oven and cook for about 20 minutes, until golden brown.

ONION BAKED POTATO ⓒ, ⒣ⓣ, ⓥ

Serves 1, Calories: 360

1 × 225 g/8 oz potato
1 large onion, unpeeled
7 g/¼ oz butter
salt and freshly ground black pepper

Scrub the potato, then prick it in several places to allow the steam to escape, and bake at 230°C/450°F/Gas Mark 8 for about 45 minutes. Now add the onion and bake for a further 45 minutes, or until the potato and onion are tender when pierced with a sharp knife. Remove them from the oven. Holding the potato in a cloth, cut it in half horizontally, then scoop the potato out of the skins without damaging them. Scoop the onion flesh out of its skin, chop the flesh and add it to the potato. Mash them together with the butter and some salt and pepper to taste. Then pile the mixture back into the potato skins, and cook for a further 10 minutes until golden brown.

PARMESAN POTATO BAKE

Serves 4, Calories per serving: 270

1 kg/2 lb potatoes
2 onions, peeled and sliced
50 g/2 oz fresh Parmesan cheese, grated
salt and freshly ground black pepper
200 ml/7 fl oz vegetable stock or water

Preheat the oven to 200°C/400°F/Gas Mark 6. Peel the potatoes and slice them as thinly as possible. Put a third of the potato slices into a shallow casserole dish and cover with half the onions and a third of the cheese. Season with salt and pepper, then follow with another layer of potato, onion, cheese and seasoning. Top with the remaining potatoes and cheese, then pour the stock or water into the dish and press the potatoes down with the back of a spoon so that they are just above the level of the water. Bake for 1½ hours, or until the potatoes are tender and the top golden brown and crisp.

VARIATIONS

POTATO BAKE Ⓒ ⒣ⓣ Ⓥ

For a non-dairy version, simply leave out the cheese. This version gives 210 Calories per serving.

CREAMY POTATO BAKE ©

Leave out the cheese and stock. Instead, pour 150 ml/5 fl oz single cream over the potatoes. Cover for the first 1 hour of baking, then uncover for the last 30 minutes to brown the top.

This version gives 300 Calories per serving.

PARSLEY POTATO CAKES ©, ⒽⓉ, Ⓥ

Serves 4 (2 cakes each)
Calories per cake: 180

1 kg/2 lb potatoes, peeled and cut into even-sized pieces
15 g/½ oz butter
1 tablespoon lemon juice
2 tablespoons chopped parsley
freshly grated nutmeg
salt and freshly ground black pepper
2 tablespoons flour, for coating
3 tablespoons olive oil

Boil the potatoes for about 20 minutes until tender, then drain, keeping the water. Mash the potatoes with the butter and the lemon juice, adding enough of the reserved water to make a firm mixture. Add the parsley, and season with nutmeg, salt and pepper. Form the mixture into round potato cakes and coat with flour. Heat the oil and fry the cakes until brown and crisp on both sides. Drain on kitchen paper.

Note: for a food-combiners' version omit the lemon juice.

PULSE AND NUT DISHES
Pulse Dishes

LENTIL BAKE (HT), (P), (V)

Serves 4, Calories per serving: 280

225 g/8 oz split red lentils
1 onion, peeled and chopped
1 tablespoon olive oil
juice of ½ lemon
salt and freshly ground black pepper
50 g/2 oz Cheddar cheese, grated
1 tomato, sliced

Preheat the oven to 180°C/350°F/Gas Mark 4.

Put the lentils into a saucepan with 450 ml/15 fl oz water and simmer over a moderate heat for 15 minutes, until tender. Meanwhile, fry the onion in the oil for 10 minutes, until soft. Mix together the lentils, onion and lemon juice, and season with salt and pepper. Put the mixture into a shallow casserole dish, top with the grated cheese and tomato slices, and bake for 20 minutes, or until the cheese is golden brown.

Note: if you are on the food-combining diet, this dish is suitable for occasional use, but omit the cheese, and serve with cooked vegetables or a salad.

LENTIL DAL (HT), (P), (V)

Serves 4, Calories per serving: 190

225 g/8 oz split red lentils
1 onion, peeled and sliced
1 bayleaf
1 whole fresh green chilli, de-seeded and chopped
(see page 155)
2.5 cm/1 in fresh ginger, grated
1 teaspoon ground turmeric
2 teaspoons ground cumin
2 teaspoons ground coriander
salt and freshly ground black pepper

Put the lentils into a saucepan with the onion, bayleaf, chilli, ginger, turmeric, and enough cold water to just cover. Bring to the boil, then cover and simmer very gently for 20–30 minutes, until the lentils and onion are tender. Remove from the heat and stir in the cumin and coriander, then cover and leave to stand for 20–30 minutes (or longer) to allow the flavours to develop. Stir well – the mixture should be creamy, add more water if necessary – and season with salt and pepper.

BUTTERBEANS BAKED WITH A HERBY TOPPING (HT), (V)

Serves 4, Calories per serving: 330

2 tablespoons olive oil
1 large onion, peeled and sliced
1 garlic clove, peeled and crushed
2 × 400 g/14 oz cans butterbeans
salt and freshly ground black pepper

100 g/4 oz breadcrumbs
1–2 tablespoons chopped fresh herbs

Heat half the oil in a large saucepan and add the onion. Fry gently for 10 minutes, until the onion has softened, then add the garlic and cook for a few moments longer. Add the butterbeans, and their liquid, and allow to heat through. Season with salt and pepper. Pour the mixture into a shallow casserole dish. Mix the breadcrumbs with the herbs and the remaining oil, rubbing the oil in lightly with your fingertips to distribute it, then sprinkle this mixture evenly on top of the butterbeans. Place under a moderate grill until heated through and crisp on top, or bake in a preheated oven at 200°C/400°F/Gas Mark 6, for 20–30 minutes.

CANNELLINI BEAN, ONION AND GARLIC STEW (HT), (P), (V)

Serves 4, Calories per serving: 200

1 tablespoon olive oil
2 large onions, peeled and sliced
2 garlic cloves, peeled and crushed
2 × 400 g/14 oz cans cannellini beans
salt and freshly ground black pepper
1–2 tablespoons chopped fresh herbs (such as
parsley and thyme)

Heat the oil in a large saucepan and add the onion. Fry gently for 10 minutes, until the onion has softened, then add the garlic and cook for a few moments longer. Add the cannellini beans, and their liquid, and allow to heat through. Season with salt and pepper, add the fresh herbs, and serve.

SPICY BEANBURGERS Ⓥ

Makes 8, Calories in each: 180
Served in a burger bun: 320 Calories

1 tablespoon olive oil
1 onion, peeled and chopped
1 carrot, finely chopped or grated
½ green pepper, de-seeded and chopped
1 garlic clove, peeled and crushed
¼–½ teaspoon hot chilli powder (optional)
1 teaspoon ground coriander
2 × 400 g/14 oz cans red kidney beans
50 g/2 oz soft wholewheat breadcrumbs
salt and freshly ground black pepper
100 g/4 oz dried wholewheat breadcrumbs, to coat
a little extra olive oil

Preheat the oven to 200°C/400°F/Gas Mark 6.

Heat the oil in a large saucepan, add the onion and stir. Cover and leave to cook over a moderate heat for 5 minutes, stirring occasionally. Then add the carrot, green pepper and garlic, and cook for a further 5 minutes. Add the spices, stir for 1–2 minutes, then remove from the heat. Mash the beans and add to the onion mixture, together with the breadcrumbs and seasoning to taste. Divide into 8, form into burgers and coat with dried breadcrumbs. Place on an oiled baking sheet and bake until brown and crisp on one side, then turn over to cook the other side. Drain on kitchen paper. Serve hot, or warm.

CHILLI LENTIL LOAF ⓗⓣ, ⓥ

Serves 4, Calories per serving: 280

175 g/6 oz brown or green lentils
1 medium onion, peeled and finely chopped
1 tablespoon olive oil
1 green chilli, de-seeded and finely chopped (see
page 155)
100 g/4 oz soft stale wholemeal breadcrumbs
2 tablespoons chopped parsley
1 tablespoon soy sauce
salt and freshly ground black pepper
3–4 tablespoons dried breadcrumbs, to coat

Preheat the oven to 190°C/375°F/Gas Mark 5.

Put the lentils into a saucepan with 3 times their volume in water and boil for about 45 minutes, until tender. Drain well and mash to break them up. Meanwhile, fry the onion in the oil for 6–7 minutes, then add the chilli and fry for 2–3 minutes longer. Add the lentils, wholemeal breadcrumbs, parsley and soy sauce. Mix well and season with salt and pepper to taste. Form into a loaf shape, coat in dried breadcrumbs and lift into a lightly oiled tin using a spatula or fish-slice if necessary. Bake for 30–40 minutes, until crisp. Cut in thick slices to serve, perhaps with tomato coulis (page 180) or yogurt and herbs (page 179).

EASY CHILLI (HT), (P), (V)

Serves 4, Calories per serving: 200

1 tablespoon olive oil
1 onion, peeled and sliced
2 garlic cloves, peeled and crushed
1 small fresh red chilli pepper, de-seeded and
sliced (see page 155)
1 small fresh green chilli pepper, de-seeded and
sliced (see page 155)
1 red pepper, de-seeded and sliced
2 × 400 g/14 oz cans red kidney beans
450 g/1 lb tomatoes, skinned and chopped
salt and freshly ground black pepper

Heat the oil in a large saucepan and add the onion. Fry
gently for 5 minutes, then add the garlic, chillis and red
pepper and cook for a further 5–10 minutes, until the red
pepper has softened. Now add the beans, with their
liquid, and the tomatoes. Simmer gently for about 5
minutes, to heat the tomatoes, then season with salt and
pepper, and serve.

Nut Dishes

HAZELNUT ROAST Ⓒ, Ⓥ

Serves 6, Calories per serving: 260

This nut roast is easy to make and is moist and delicious either hot or cold.

1 onion, peeled and chopped
1 tablespoon olive oil
2 carrots, peeled and grated
1 stick of celery, finely chopped
2 teaspoons wholemeal flour
1 teaspoon dried rosemary
200 g/7 oz wholemeal breadcrumbs
200 g/7 oz grated or crushed hazelnuts
1 teaspoon yeast extract
2 tablespoons tamari or other soy sauce
salt and freshly ground black pepper
2–3 tablespoons dried breadcrumbs, to coat

Preheat the oven to 200°C/400°F/Gas Mark 6.

Fry the onion in the oil for 5 minutes until tender, then add the carrots and celery, and cook for a further 5 minutes. Add the flour and 300 ml/10 fl oz water, and stir over the heat until slightly thickened. Remove from the heat and add the rosemary, breadcrumbs, hazelnuts, yeast extract, tamari and some salt and pepper to taste. Form into a loaf shape, coat in the dried breadcrumbs and place in a lightly oiled tin. Bake for 30–40 minutes, until crisp. Cut in thick slices to serve.

A sauce, such as tomato coulis (page 180) or yogurt and herbs (page 179), goes well with this.

SMOKED TOFU WITH HAZELNUTS ⒣, Ⓟ, Ⓥ

Serves 2, Calories per serving: 180

This recipe may seem strange, but it is a curiously pleasant mixture of flavours. Serve with stir-fried vegetables.

225 g/8 oz smoked tofu, drained
50 g/2 oz hazelnuts
2 tablespoons soy sauce
1 garlic clove, peeled and crushed
½ teaspoon honey
salt and freshly ground black pepper

Cut the tofu in half vertically, then slice both pieces in half horizontally (these halves will later be sandwiched together). Leave on one side for a moment.

Grind the hazelnuts, then mix with the soy sauce, garlic and honey, to make a paste (or whizz them all in the food processor – no need to crush the garlic first). Season with salt and pepper, then sandwich the slices of tofu together with this mixture, and cut across into smaller pieces. Grill or microwave until heated through.

NUT BURGER-FOR-ONE Ⓥ

Makes 1, Calories: 300

Measure the peanut butter carefully – make sure the tablespoon is level, not rounded – to keep to the Calorie count given.

1 onion, peeled and finely chopped
2 teaspoons oil

25 g/1 oz fresh wholemeal breadcrumbs
1 tablespoon crunchy peanut butter
2 teaspoons soy sauce
salt and freshly ground black pepper

Fry the onion in half the oil for 10 minutes until tender, then remove from the heat and add the breadcrumbs, peanut butter and soy sauce. Season to taste with salt and pepper, mix well, then form into a burger shape. Heat the rest of the oil in a small frying pan and fry the burger for about 3 minutes on each side, until brown and crisp on the outside and hot inside.

FLANS AND PIES

FRESH ASPARAGUS AND MUSHROOMS IN FILO BASKETS Ⓒ, ⒣⒯

Serves 6, Calories per serving: 130

25 g/1 oz butter
3 sheets of filo pastry (each about 45 × 30 cm/18 × 12 in)
225 g/8 oz asparagus, washed and trimmed
1 garlic clove, peeled and crushed
350 g/12 oz button mushrooms, washed and sliced
1 teaspoon cornflour
6 tablespoons single cream
salt and freshly ground black pepper

Preheat the oven to 190°C/375°F/Gas Mark 5 and brush 6 individual ramekin dishes lightly with some of the butter, making sure to grease the rims too.

Cut each piece of filo pastry in half lengthwise and then into 3 crosswise, to make 6 pieces. Put three pieces into a pile, then rearrange them so that the corners are staggered to look like the petals of a flower. Put each pile of filo squares into one of the ramekins, pushing them down gently. Bake for about 15 minutes, until lightly browned. Then gently ease the cases out of the ramekins and turn them upside down on a baking sheet. Return them to the oven for a few more minutes to brown the undersides.

Meanwhile, make the filling. Cook the asparagus in a little boiling water for about 7 minutes, until just tender, then drain and cut into 2.5 cm/1 in pieces. Heat the remaining butter in a saucepan and fry the garlic for a few moments, then add the mushrooms and fry for 5 minutes, until tender. Add the asparagus to the mushrooms and stir-fry until all the vegetables are hot. Blend the cornflour with the cream and add to the vegetables; stir for a few minutes until thickened. Season with salt and pepper to taste. Spoon this mixture into the filo cases and serve at once.

FRENCH ONION QUICHE ©

Serves 6, Calories per serving: 300

450 g/1 lb onions, peeled and very thinly sliced
1 tablespoon olive oil
150 g/5 oz self-raising 81% wholewheat flour
¼ teaspoon salt
75 g/3 oz butter
2 egg yolks
150 ml/5 fl oz single cream
salt and freshly ground black pepper
freshly grated nutmeg

First make a start on the filling. Fry the onions very gently in the oil in a large saucepan for about 30 minutes, or until very tender but not browned. Stir often to prevent sticking. Remove from the heat. While the onions are cooking, preheat the oven to 190°C/375°F/Gas Mark 5.

To make the pastry, put the flour into a bowl with the salt. Rub in the butter with your fingertips until the mixture looks like fine breadcrumbs. Gather the mixture together to make a dough. It should hold together well because of the slightly higher than usual proportion of fat, but add a few drops of cold water to help bind it if necessary. Roll the pastry out on a lightly floured board and use to line a 20 cm/8 in flan tin; trim the edges.

Now whisk the egg yolks and cream together, and season with salt, pepper and nutmeg. Put the onions into the flan case and pour the egg mixture over the top. Bake for 35–40 minutes, or until the pastry is crisp and the filling set and lightly browned. Serve hot or warm.

VARIATIONS

BROCCOLI QUICHE ©
Omit the onions and the oil, and use 350 g/12 oz broccoli instead. Trim the broccoli and break it into florets, then steam or boil until just tender. Drain well. This version serves 6 and gives 290 Calories per serving.

MUSHROOM QUICHE ©
Use 350 g/12 oz sliced button mushrooms instead of the onions. Fry them in the oil for 4–5 minutes, until just tender. (If they make a great deal of liquid, boil them hard until it has all disappeared.) This version serves 6 and gives 290 Calories per serving.

LEEK QUICHE ©

Use 450 g/1 lb leeks, washed and sliced, instead of the onions. This version serves 6 and gives 300 Calories per serving.

GREEK SPINACH PIE

Serves 4–6
Calories per serving for 6: 220
Calories per serving for 4: 330

1 kg/2 lb fresh spinach, or 450 g/1 lb frozen leaf
spinach
100 g/4 oz Feta cheese, crumbled
1 onion, peeled and finely chopped
2 tablespoons chopped fresh herbs, including
fennel if possible
salt and freshly ground black pepper
6 sheets of filo pastry (each about 45 × 30 cm/18 ×
12 in)
40 g/1½ oz butter, melted

Preheat the oven to 190°C/375°F/Gas Mark 5.

Wash the fresh spinach thoroughly and cook in a large saucepan without extra water for about 10 minutes, until tender. If using frozen spinach, put into a pan half-filled with boiling water and cook for a few minutes until tender. In either case, drain very thoroughly and put into a bowl with the cheese, onion, fresh herbs, and salt and pepper to taste.

Cut the sheets of filo pastry in half crosswise. Put one in the base of a shallow ovenproof dish. Brush lightly with butter, then put another piece on top, and repeat with 2 more pieces, brushing each with butter before putting the next on top. Then spoon in the filling. Cover with the remaining 8 sheets of pastry, brushing each with melted butter. Then bake for about 50 minutes, until golden brown. Serve with Yogurt and Herb Dip (page 179) and a Greek Salad (page 160), or a cooked vegetable.

VARIATION

FOOD-COMBINERS' GREEK SPINACH PIE
Ⓒ, ⒣⒯, Ⓥ

Omit the cheese. This version gives 190 Calories if serving 6; 280 Calories if serving 4.

EGG AND CHEESE DISHES

MUSHROOM OMELETTE Ⓟ

Serves 1, Calories: 280

15 g/½ oz butter
50 g/2 oz mushrooms, sliced
2 eggs
salt and freshly ground black pepper

Melt half the butter in a small saucepan, fry the mushrooms lightly until tender and keep warm. Next, crack the eggs into a bowl, season with salt and pepper, and beat lightly, just to combine (don't beat them too much). Put the frying pan over a moderate to high heat for a few minutes, to heat up, then melt the rest of the butter and pour in the eggs. Stir the eggs gently with a fork, and as the bottom begins to set draw it back with a spatula and tip the pan to allow the unset egg to run on to the hot pan.

When the omelette is almost set, put the mushrooms on top. Hold the frying pan up by its handle at right angles to a warmed plate. Using a spatula, roll the top third of the omelette down, and at the same time tip the frying pan over the plate, so that the omelette rolls and comes out of the pan on to the plate, fold-side down. Serve immediately.

VARIATION

ASPARAGUS OMELETTE Ⓟ

Make as above, using 2 fat asparagus spears instead of the mushrooms, and only half the butter. Prepare the asparagus by removing the tough stalk ends, chopping the stems into 2.5 cm/1 in lengths and cooking them in a little fast-boiling water for 5–7 minutes, until just tender. This version gives 290 Calories.

CHEESY OAT AND TOMATO BAKE

Serves 2, Calories per serving: 280

450 g/1 lb tomatoes, skinned and chopped
¼–½ teaspoon dried oregano or basil
salt and freshly ground black pepper
25 g/1 oz rolled porridge oats
25 g/1 oz Cheddar cheese, grated

Preheat the oven to 200°C/400°F/Gas Mark 6.

Put the tomatoes into a shallow casserole dish and sprinkle with 4 tablespoons water, the dried herbs, and salt and pepper to taste. Scatter the oats and cheese evenly on top. Bake for about 20 minutes, until the topping is crisp and golden.

CHEESE FRITTERS

Serves 4, Calories per serving: 300

450 ml/15 fl oz skimmed milk or soya milk
1 small onion, peeled and stuck with 1 clove
1 bayleaf
75 g/3 oz semolina
50 g/2 oz Parmesan cheese, grated
1–2 tablespoons chopped parsley
½ teaspoon mustard powder
salt and freshly ground black pepper
1 large egg, beaten with 1 tablespoon water
dried breadcrumbs, to coat
oil, to shallow-fry

Put the milk, onion and bayleaf in a large saucepan. Bring to the boil, then remove from the heat, cover and leave for 10–15 minutes, to allow the flavours to infuse. When infused, remove and discard the onion and bayleaf. Bring the milk to the boil again, then gradually sprinkle the semolina over the top, stirring all the time. Let the mixture simmer for about 5 minutes, stirring often, to cook the semolina. Remove from the heat and beat in two-thirds of the cheese, the parsley, mustard and seasoning.

Brush a large plate or baking sheet with oil. Turn the semolina mixture out on to this and spread out to about 1 cm/½ in deep all over. Smooth the surface, then leave to cool completely. It will get firm as it cools. Cut into triangles and dip these first in the beaten egg, then in the dried breadcrumbs, to coat completely.

Heat 5 mm/¼ in oil in a frying pan, and fry the cheese fritters for about 4 minutes on each side, or until crisp and golden brown. Leave to drain very well on kitchen paper. Serve with lemon slices.

SPINACH ROULADE Ⓟ

Serves 4–6
Calories per serving for 6: 200
Calories per serving for 4: 300

4–6 tablespoons grated Parmesan cheese
450 g/1 lb frozen spinach or 1 kg/2 lb fresh
spinach, cooked and drained
25 g/1 oz butter
4 eggs, separated
salt and freshly ground black pepper
freshly grated nutmeg
225 g/8 oz quark

Preheat the oven to 190°C/375°F/Gas Mark 5, line a 23 ×
33 cm/9 × 13 in swiss roll tin with greaseproof paper,
grease generously with butter and sprinkle with 2–3
tablespoons Parmesan cheese.

Using your hands, squeeze as much water as you can
from the spinach, then chop it fairly finely. You should
have about 225 g/8 oz cooked chopped spinach. Put the
spinach in a saucepan with the butter and cook gently
until heated through. Then remove from the heat and add
the egg yolks, stirring thoroughly. Whisk the egg whites
until stiff but not dry, and fold them into the spinach
mixture. Season with salt, pepper and nutmeg. Spoon the
mixture into the tin, making sure it goes into the corners,
and level gently with the back of the spoon.

Bake for about 15–20 minutes, until puffed up, golden
brown and set in the middle. Have ready a damp tea
towel, spread with a large piece of greaseproof paper
sprinkled with the remaining Parmesan. Turn the roulade
out on to the paper and strip the lining paper off its top

surface. Beat the quark to soften it, then spread it evenly over the roulade. Now gently roll up the roulade, from one of the long edges, and trim the ends with a sharp serrated knife. Lift it on to a flat heatproof dish and put into the oven for 5–10 minutes to heat through. Serve immediately, perhaps with a tomato coulis (page 180).

GOAT'S CHEESE ON TOMATO SLICES Ⓗⓣ, Ⓟ

Serves 2, Calories per serving: 130

**100 g/4 oz log-shaped goat's cheese
3 tomatoes (the same circumference as the goat's cheese or a little bigger)
freshly ground black pepper**

Cut the goat's cheese into 8 circles. Slice the tomatoes, to make 8 thick circles, too. Put the tomato slices on to a grill pan or heatproof dish and top each with a circle of goat's cheese and some freshly ground black pepper. Grill until the cheese is beginning to melt and go brown, but the tomato is still fairly firm. Serve at once. This goes well with the Cabbage, Apple and Sage Salad (page 163).

PASTA AND RICE DISHES
Pasta

FETTUCINE WITH RED PEPPER Ⓒ, Ⓥ

Serves 4
Calories per serving, without soured cream: 270
Calories per serving, with soured cream: 300

225 g/8 oz fettucine
1 tablespoon olive oil
2 garlic cloves, peeled and crushed
2 red peppers, de-seeded and cut into thin strips
8 spring onions, cut into thin strips
1 teaspoon black peppercorns, crushed
4 tablespoons soured cream (optional)

Cook the fettucine in a large saucepan of boiling water for
8–10 minutes, until just tender, then drain. Meanwhile,
heat the oil and fry the garlic for 2–3 minutes, then add
the peppers and spring onions and stir-fry for 3–4 minutes. Season with salt and add the vegetables and crushed
peppercorns to the pasta. Serve the pasta in warmed
individual bowls, top each with a swirl of soured cream if
using, and serve immediately.

FETTUCINE WITH MUSHROOMS IN CREAM SAUCE ©

Serves 4, Calories per serving: 340

225 g/8 oz fettucine or tagliatelle
750 g/1½ lb button mushrooms
15 g/½ oz butter
1 garlic clove, peeled and crushed
1 teaspoon cornflour
150 ml/5 fl oz single cream
salt and freshly ground black pepper
freshly grated nutmeg
chopped parsley, to serve

First heat up a large saucepan of water for the pasta. When the water reaches the boil, remove from the heat and add 1 teaspoon salt. Then put in the pasta and cook, uncovered, until just tender (3–4 minutes for fresh pasta or 8–10 minutes for dried – be guided by timings given with the pasta).

While the pasta is cooking, make the sauce. Wash and slice the mushrooms, then fry them in the butter with the crushed garlic until they are tender and all the liquid they produce has boiled away. Stir in the cornflour, then add the cream and stir over the heat for a few minutes until slightly thickened. Season with salt, pepper and nutmeg. Drain the pasta carefully, then serve out on to warmed plates, spoon the mushroom mixture on top and sprinkle with chopped parsley.

TAGLIATELLE WITH CREAM AND BROCCOLI ©

Serves 4, Calories per serving: 290

350 g/12 oz broccoli
100 ml/3½ fl oz single cream
225 g/8 oz tagliatelle
salt and freshly ground black pepper
freshly grated nutmeg

First heat up a large saucepan of water for the pasta.
Meanwhile, prepare the broccoli: remove the tough stalk
ends and cut into thin matchsticks, then break the florets
into small pieces. Cook the broccoli in a little fast-boiling
water for about 4 minutes, until just tender, then drain
and add the cream. Cook the pasta in the boiling water
until just tender (3–4 minutes for fresh pasta or 8–10
minutes for dried – be guided by timings given with the
pasta). Drain the pasta carefully, then add the broccoli
mixture and season to taste with salt, pepper and nutmeg.
Mix gently over a low heat until warmed through, and
serve.

VARIATIONS

TAGLIATELLE WITH ASPARAGUS ©

For this luxury summer dish, use 350 g/12 oz asparagus
instead of the broccoli. Remove and discard the tough
stalk ends, and cut the asparagus into 2.5 cm/1 in lengths
before cooking. This version gives 290 Calories.

TAGLIATELLE WITH SPRING VEGETABLES ©

Use 350 g/12 oz tiny tender spring vegetables – choose
from French beans, baby carrots, young courgettes and

mangetout – instead of broccoli. Trim and boil or steam very lightly. This version gives 290 Calories.

SPAGHETTI WITH TOMATO SAUCE Ⓥ
Serves 4
Calories per serving, without Parmesan: 300
Calories per serving, with 1 tablespoon Parmesan: 330

450 g/1 lb tomatoes, or 1 × 425 g/15 oz can
tomatoes
1 tablespoon olive oil
1 onion, peeled and chopped
1 teaspoon dried basil
1 large garlic clove, peeled and crushed
salt and freshly ground black pepper
225 g/8 oz spaghetti
15 g/½ oz butter
4 tablespoons grated Parmesan cheese (optional)

First heat up a large saucepan of water for the pasta.

Meanwhile, make the sauce. Peel the tomatoes by putting them into a bowl, covering with boiling water and leaving for 1–2 minutes, then slipping off the skins with a pointed knife. Chop the tomatoes roughly. If using canned tomatoes, just chop these. Next, heat the oil in a medium-sized saucepan and fry the onion for 5 minutes with a lid on the pan. Add the tomatoes, basil and garlic, mix well, then cover and simmer for 15–20 minutes. Season with salt and pepper.

Cook the spaghetti in the boiling water, uncovered, for 8–10 minutes, or until just tender. Gently drain the pasta, then return it to the saucepan with the butter and some salt and pepper. Serve it out into warmed dishes, pour the sauce on top and sprinkle with grated Parmesan if liked.

PIMENTO LASAGNE

Serves 8, Calories per serving: 210

It's very helpful to have a food processor for this recipe, for chopping the carrots and peppers.

1 tablespoon olive oil
1 onion, peeled and chopped
2 garlic cloves, peeled and crushed
450 g/1 lb carrots, scraped and grated or finely chopped in a food processor
3 red peppers, de-seeded and very finely chopped in a food processor
1 × 425 g/15 oz can tomatoes, puréed in a food processor
2 tablespoons tomato purée
salt and freshly ground black pepper
9 sheets of ready-to-use lasagne verde (about 175 g/6 oz)

For the cheese sauce

15 g/½ oz butter
15 g/½ oz cornflour
600 ml/1 pint skimmed milk
1 teaspoon mustard powder
50 g/2 oz Parmesan cheese, grated
salt and freshly ground black pepper

Preheat the oven to 200°C/400°F/Gas Mark 6.

Heat the oil in a medium-sized saucepan and fry the onion for 5 minutes, then add the garlic, carrots, red peppers, tomatoes and tomato purée. Stir well, then cover and cook gently for 20–30 minutes, until all the vegetables are tender. Season with salt and pepper. Cover the bottom of a lightly oiled shallow casserole dish with pieces of lasagne. Spoon half the pepper mixture on top, then put more sheets of pasta on top, followed by the rest of the pepper mixture and a final layer of lasagne.

Make the cheese sauce by melting the butter in a saucepan and stirring in the cornflour. Cook for a few moments, then add the milk in several batches, stirring well after each addition, and adding more when the mixture thickens. Cook for 2 minutes, remove from the heat, and add the mustard powder, half the cheese and plenty of salt and pepper to taste. Pour this sauce over the top of the lasagne and sprinkle with the remaining Parmesan. Bake for 40 minutes, until golden brown and bubbling hot.

MACARONI 'CHEESE' Ⓒ

Serves 4, Calories per serving: 310

This is a compatible-eating version of macaroni cheese. It contains neither cheese nor milk, so can be enjoyed as a carbohydrate meal if you're food-combining. We prefer it to traditional macaroni cheese.

150 g/5 oz quick-cook or wholewheat macaroni
25 g/1 oz butter
25 g/1 oz flour
600 ml/1 pint water
1 teaspoon Dijon mustard
150 ml/5 fl oz soured cream
salt and freshly ground black pepper
40 g/1½ oz soft fresh wholewheat breadcrumbs

Heat the grill or preheat the oven to 200°C/400°F/Gas Mark 6.

Bring a large saucepan of water to the boil, put in the macaroni and cook, uncovered, for 8–10 minutes, or until just tender. Next, make a sauce by melting the butter in a saucepan and stirring in the flour. Cook for a few moments, then add the water in several batches, stirring well after each addition, and adding more when the mixture thickens. Cook for 5 minutes, remove from the heat, and add the mustard, the soured cream and plenty of salt and pepper to taste.

Drain the macaroni and mix it with the sauce. Check the seasoning, then put the mixture into a casserole dish. Sprinkle the breadcrumbs on top, place the dish under the preheated grill for about 10 minutes to heat through and crisp the top; or bake in the oven for 15–20 minutes until hot inside and brown and crisp on top.

Rice

MUSHROOM RISOTTO Ⓥ

Serves 6, Calories per serving: 270
Calories per serving, with 1 tablespoon Parmesan: 300

1 tablespoon olive oil
1 onion, peeled and chopped
350 g/12 oz rice
300 ml/10 fl oz tomato juice
3 tomatoes, skinned and chopped
225 g/8 oz button mushrooms, wiped and sliced
salt and freshly ground black pepper
freshly chopped parsley, to serve
6 tablespoons Parmesan cheese, grated (optional)

Heat the oil in a large saucepan and fry the onion gently for 5 minutes, then add the rice and stir over the heat for 2–3 minutes. Add 225 ml/7½ fl oz water and simmer, stirring often, until the water has been absorbed by the rice. Then add another 225 ml/7½ fl oz water and the tomato juice. Cover and cook, stirring occasionally (20 minutes for white rice, 30 minutes for brown). Now add the tomatoes and mushrooms and cook for a further 10 minutes, or until the rice is tender. If there is liquid left, stir over a high heat until all the liquid has been absorbed. Season with salt and pepper, then turn into a heated serving dish and sprinkle with chopped parsley. Hand round the Parmesan cheese separately.

Note: food-combiners can replace the tomato juice with water and omit the tomatoes for a carbohydrate dish.

VARIATIONS

LEEK RISOTTO Ⓥ
Use 225 g/8 oz chopped leeks, steamed until just tender, instead of the mushrooms. This version gives 280 Calories per serving.

ASPARAGUS RISOTTO Ⓥ
Use 225 g/8 oz asparagus instead of the mushrooms. Cut off the tough stalk ends, then cut the asparagus into 2.5 cm/1 in lengths. Add with the tomatoes. This version gives 270 Calories per serving.

MUSHROOMS IN CREAM ON BROWN RICE ©

Serves 4, Calories per serving: 330

225 g/8 oz brown rice
1 teaspoon salt
½ teaspoon turmeric
750 g/1½ lb button mushrooms
15 g/½ oz butter
1 garlic clove, peeled and crushed
1 teaspoon cornflour
150 ml/5 fl oz single cream
salt and freshly ground black pepper
freshly grated nutmeg
chopped parsley, to serve

Put the rice into a saucepan with the salt, turmeric and 600 ml/1 pint water. Bring to the boil, then cover, turn the heat down low, and leave to cook gently for 45 minutes.

Meanwhile, wash and slice the mushrooms, then fry them in the butter with the garlic until they are tender and all the liquid they produce has boiled away. Stir in the cornflour, then add the cream and stir over the heat for a few minutes until slightly thickened. Season with salt, pepper and nutmeg. Make a border of the rice on a serving dish or 4 individual plates and spoon the mushroom mixture inside it. Sprinkle with chopped parsley.

PUDDINGS AND FRUIT SALADS
Puddings

CHOCOLATE ICE-CREAM ⓥ

Serves 8, Calories per serving: 200

100 g/4 oz plain chocolate, broken into pieces
900 ml/1½ pints skimmed or soya milk
1 tablespoon cornflour
25 g/1 oz sugar
300 ml/10 fl oz single cream, evaporated milk or
concentrated soya milk (e.g. Plamil)

Put the chocolate pieces into a saucepan with almost all
the milk and bring to the boil. Blend the cornflour and
sugar to a paste in a bowl with the remaining milk. Add a
little of the chocolate and milk mixture to the cornflour
mixture, blend, then pour the cornflour mixture into the
saucepan. Stir over a moderate heat for 2–3 minutes, until
slightly thickened. Remove from the heat. Cool slightly,
then add the single cream, evaporated milk or concentrated soya milk and liquidise until smooth. Pour into a
polythene container, allow to cool completely, then
freeze, beating once during freezing. This ice-cream
freezes hard; remove from the freezer to room temperature
30–40 minutes before eating.

TOFU STRAWBERRY ICE-CREAM (HT), (V)

Serves 4, Calories per serving: 120

Silken tofu, which you can buy in a vacuum pack, is best for this if you can get it; if not, the ordinary, firmer tofu will do. This is a wonderful, thick, creamy ice-cream, relatively low in Calories and with no cholesterol! However you do need a food processor, and you do need to start a few hours in advance in order to freeze the fruit.

225 g/8 oz fresh strawberries, washed, hulled, and large ones halved or quartered
1 large banana, peeled and cut into 1 cm/½ in chunks
275 g/10 oz tofu, preferably silken
4 tablespoons clear honey
½ teaspoon vanilla essence
4 small strawberries, green stalks still attached, to decorate

Put the strawberries and banana chunks on a plate in a single layer and freeze until just before you want to serve the dish. Then put them into a food processor with the tofu, honey and vanilla essence. Whizz to a smooth purée – it will make a thick, creamy ice-cream. Spoon into individual glasses, top each with a small strawberry, and serve immediately.

VARIATIONS

Many different fruits can be used instead of the strawberries.

TOFU PEACH ICE-CREAM (HT), (V)
Use 2 large peaches, skinned, stoned and cut into

1 cm/½ in pieces, instead of the strawberries. This version gives 130 Calories per serving.

TOFU MANGO ICE-CREAM (HT), (V)
Use 1 large ripe mango, skinned, stoned and cut into 1 cm/½ in pieces instead of the strawberries. This version gives 130 Calories per serving.

TOFU RASPBERRY ICE-CREAM (HT), (V)
Use 225 g/8 oz raspberries instead of the strawberries. This version gives 120 Calories per serving.

TOFU FRUIT FOOL (HT), (V)
Serves 4, Calories per serving: 130

**1 banana
275 g/10 oz silken tofu
1 tablespoon clear honey or caster sugar
½ teaspoon vanilla essence**

Peel and chop the banana. Put it into a food processor with the tofu, honey or sugar and vanilla essence. Whizz to a smooth purée. Spoon into individual glasses.

VARIATION
TOFU AND PEACH FOOL (HT), (V)
Add a large peach, skinned, stoned and chopped, to the tofu, along with the banana. This version gives 140 Calories per serving.

TOFU VANILLA CREAM Ⓗⓣ, Ⓥ

Serves 4–8, Calories per serving for 4: 80

**1 large banana, peeled and cut into 1 cm/½ in
chunks
275 g/10 oz tofu, preferably silken
2 tablespoons clear honey
½ teaspoon vanilla essence**

Put the banana chunks on a plate in a single layer and
freeze until just before you want to serve the dish. Then
put them into a food processor with the tofu, honey and
vanilla essence. Whizz to a smooth, thick, creamy purée
and serve immediately, either in individual dishes, as a
pudding or for breakfast, or spooned on top of fresh fruit
salad.

PINEAPPLE AND ORANGE SORBET Ⓗⓣ, Ⓥ

*Serves 4
Calories per serving, without Cointreau: 130
Calories per serving, with Cointreau: 140*

**1 medium ripe pineapple
2 oranges, squeezed, to make about 200 ml/7 fl oz
juice
25 g/1 oz caster sugar
1 tablespoon Cointreau (optional)**

Peel the pineapple and cut the flesh into chunks. Liquidise
these with the orange juice, sugar, and Cointreau if using.
Put into a suitable container and freeze until firm. Remove from the freezer 20–30 minutes before serving,
then break up and whisk by hand, or in a food processor,

until light and fluffy. Serve immediately, in individual glasses.

VARIATIONS

PINEAPPLE AND PASSION FRUIT SORBET (HT), (V)
Use the same basic mixture, but add the pulp and seeds of 2 passion fruit as well. This version gives 150 Calories per serving.

MANGO SORBET (HT), (V)
Use a large ripe mango, peeled and stoned, instead of the pineapple. This version gives 170 Calories per serving.

BLACKBERRY SORBET (HT), (V)

Serves 4, Calories per serving: 120

75 g/3 oz granulated sugar
450 g/1 lb fresh or frozen blackberries
grated rind and juice of ½ lemon

Put 300 ml/10 fl oz water into a saucepan and add the sugar. Heat very gently until the sugar has dissolved, then raise the heat and boil rapidly for 5–6 minutes, until syrupy. Remove from the heat and cool. Meanwhile, sieve the blackberries into the syrup, and add the lemon juice and rind. Freeze until firm. Remove from the freezer 30 minutes or so before serving, then break up and whisk by hand, or in a food processor, until light and fluffy. Serve immediately, in individual glasses.

VARIATION

BLACKCURRANT SORBET (HT), (V)
Make as described, but use blackcurrants instead of the blackberries. This also gives 120 Calories per serving.

LEMON SORBET (HT)

Serves 4, Calories per serving: 120

3 lemons
100 g/4 oz caster sugar
1 egg white

Scrub the lemons, grate the rind into a saucepan and add 450 ml/15 fl oz water. Bring to the boil, then simmer for 10 minutes. Strain, add the sugar and stir until dissolved. Pour into a shallow container and freeze for 1 hour or until just firm. Whisk the egg white until stiff, then whisk in chunks of the frozen lemon syrup. Whisk until thick. Return to the container and freeze for 2 hours until firm. Remove from the freezer 45 minutes before serving.

ORANGE CHEESECAKE

Serves 8, Calories per serving: 120

2 large sweet oranges
3 wheatmeal biscuits
350 g/12 oz quark
2 eggs
40 g/1½ oz caster sugar

Preheat the oven to 180°C/350°F/Gas Mark 4.

Grate the rind from one of the oranges. Crush the biscuits and sprinkle them evenly in the base of an 18 cm/7 in loose-bottomed flan tin. Whisk together the quark, eggs, caster sugar and grated orange rind. Spread the mixture evenly over the biscuit crumb base. Bake for about 45 minutes, or until set, then remove from the oven and chill.

To serve, peel the oranges with a knife, using a sawing motion and cutting round and round as if you were peeling an apple. Remove any remaining pith, then cut the orange segments out from between the membranes. Arrange the segments on top of the cheesecake.

VARIATION

ORANGE AND STRAWBERRY CHEESECAKE
Decorate the top of the cheesecake with 350 g/12 oz hulled fresh strawberries instead of the orange segments. This version gives 130 Calories per serving.

HONEY AND RAISIN BAKED APPLES (HT), (V)

Serves 4, Calories per serving: 160

4 large cooking apples
100 g/4 oz raisins
1 tablespoon clear honey

Preheat the oven to 180°C/350°F/Gas Mark 4.

Wash the apples, then remove the cores, using an apple corer or a sharp knife and making a neat cavity. Score the skin around the middle of each apple, then place them in an ovenproof dish. Fill the centre of the apples with the raisins, pushing them in firmly. Dissolve the honey in 4 tablespoons hot water and pour round the apples. Bake for about 30 minutes, or until the apples are tender when pierced with the point of a sharp knife. Spoon some of the honey liquid over each before serving.

QUICK YOGURT PUDDING

Serves 2, Calories per serving: 190

300 ml/10 fl oz Greek yogurt
½ teaspoon ground cinnamon
½ teaspoon lemon juice
25 g/1 oz soft brown sugar

Mix together the yogurt, cinnamon and lemon juice. Spoon the mixture into a glass serving dish, or 2 individual dishes, and cover the top with an even layer of soft brown sugar. Chill until needed.

LEMON MERINGUE (HT)

Serves 4, Calories per serving: 180

50 g/2 oz cornflour
grated rind of 1 lemon
juice of 2 lemons
100 g/4 oz caster sugar
2 egg whites

Preheat the oven to 140°C/275°F/Gas Mark 1.
Put the cornflour, lemon rind and juice into a pan with half the sugar and gradually add 300 ml/10 fl oz water, stirring, to make a smooth paste. Heat gently, stirring all the time, until thickened. Remove from the heat and pour into a shallow ovenproof dish. Whisk the egg whites until stiff, then whisk in the remaining sugar. Pile this meringue on top of the lemon then spread it out to the edges. Bake for 1 hour, or until the meringue is crisp and lightly browned. Serve hot or cold.

PEARS IN WINE ⓗⓣ, Ⓥ

Serves 4, Calories per serving: 160

**4 firm dessert pears
50 g/2 oz granulated sugar
300 ml/10 fl oz red wine**

Peel the pears, leaving them whole (don't remove the stalks). Put the sugar into a saucepan with the wine and 300 ml/10 fl oz water. Heat gently until the sugar has dissolved, then bring to the boil. Add the pears, cover and simmer gently for 30–40 minutes, or until the pears are tender right through to the centres. Don't undercook them, or the insides will turn brown. When the pears are done, remove them from the pan with a slotted spoon and place them in a serving dish. Boil the liquid in the pan vigorously until reduced by half, and pour this syrup over the pears. Cool, then chill.

PEACHES IN WINE ⓗⓣ, Ⓥ

Serves 4, Calories per serving: 90

**4 large ripe peaches
25 g/1 oz caster sugar
120 ml/4 fl oz sweet white wine**

Skin the peaches by putting them into a deep bowl, covering them with boiling water and leaving for 2–3 minutes, until you can slip the skins off easily with a pointed knife. At this point drain the peaches, and remove all the skins. Slice the peaches, removing the stones. Put the slices into a glass bowl, or individual dishes, and sprinkle with the sugar. Pour over the wine, then chill for at least 30 minutes, or until needed.

Fruit Salads

ORANGE, KIWI AND LYCHEE FRUIT SALAD
(FV), (HT), (P), (V)

Serves 4, Calories per serving: 90

3 large oranges
2 kiwi fruit
1 × 400g/14 oz can lychees, drained and rinsed

Squeeze the juice from 1 of the oranges and put it into a
bowl. Holding them over the bowl, peel the remaining
oranges with a knife, using a sawing motion and cutting
round and round as if you were peeling an apple. Remove
any remaining pith, then cut the orange segments out
from between the membranes and put them into the
bowl. Peel and slice the kiwi fruit and add to the bowl
along with the lychees.

VARIATIONS

APPLE, GRAPE AND ORANGE FRUIT SALAD
(FV), (HT), (P), (V)

Omit the kiwi fruit and lychees. Instead, use 2 dessert
apples, cored and sliced, and 225 g/8 oz grapes, halved
and de-seeded. This version gives 100 Calories per serving.

MANGO, KIWI AND PAWPAW FRUIT SALAD
(FV), (HT), (P), (V)

Omit 2 of the oranges and all the lychees. Squeeze the
juice from the remaining orange and put it into a bowl.
Add the kiwi fruit, 1 mango, peeled, stoned and sliced,
and 1 ripe pawpaw, peeled, seeds removed and the flesh
sliced. This version gives 80 Calories per serving.

240

MELON, GRAPE AND KIWI FRUIT SALAD
(FV), (HT), (V)

Omit 2 of the oranges and all the lychees. Squeeze the juice from the remaining orange and put it into a bowl. Add the kiwi fruit, the diced flesh of a small Charentais or Ogen melon and 225 g/8 oz grapes, halved and de-seeded. This version gives 100 Calories per serving.

STRAWBERRY, GRAPE AND KIWI FRUIT SALAD
(FV), (HT), (P), (V)

Omit 2 of the oranges and all the lychees. Squeeze the juice from the remaining orange and put it into a bowl. Add the kiwi fruit, 225 g/8 oz strawberries and 255 g/8 oz grapes, halved and de-seeded. This version gives 80 Calories per serving.

PEAR, GRAPE AND ORANGE FRUIT SALAD
(FV), (HT), (P), (V)

Omit the kiwi fruit and lychees and add 2 ripe pears, peeled, cored and sliced, and 225 g/8 oz black or red grapes, halved and de-seeded. This version gives 100 Calories per serving.

STRAWBERRY AND ORANGE FRUIT SALAD
(FV), (HT), (P), (V)

Omit the kiwi fruit and lychees and add 450 g/1 lb hulled, washed and sliced strawberries. This version gives 70 Calories per serving.

GRAPE AND PEACH FRUIT SALAD
Ⓕⓥ, Ⓗⓣ, Ⓟ, Ⓥ

Serves 1, Calories per serving: 100

1 large ripe peach, stoned and sliced
10 sweet green grapes, halved and de-seeded
1 tablespoon single cream

Mix together the peach and grapes. Just before serving, pour the cream on top.

GREEK FRUIT SALAD Ⓕⓥ, Ⓗⓣ, Ⓟ, Ⓥ

Serves 4, Calories per serving: 120

2 ripe peaches, stoned and sliced
2 ripe figs, sliced
225 g/8 oz strawberries, hulled
2 kiwi fruit, peeled and sliced
225 g/8 oz black grapes, halved and de-seeded
2 apples, peeled, cored and sliced
juice of 1 lemon

Arrange the prepared fruits in heaps on a large plate – they look particularly good on a large white or glass plate. Sprinkle with the lemon juice. This dish is good served with some thick Greek yogurt.

Part 4
Where to Find the Nutrients

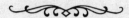

A vegetarian diet – that is, a diet which does not include meat or fish but which does include dairy produce – can supply all the nutrients needed for health and vitality. The same is true of a vegan diet, which does not include any meat, fish or dairy produce, as long as it is sensibly balanced.

The main nutrients we need are proteins, carbohydrates, fats, minerals (such as iron and calcium), mineral salts (such as zinc, sodium and potassium) and vitamins. Their function in the body, and main sources in the vegetarian/vegan diet, are listed below.

PROTEIN

Protein is essential for healthy growth and repair of body cells: too little can result in stunted growth and general poor health, but too much can interfere with our ability to absorb calcium and also puts an extra strain on the kidneys.

The main sources of protein for vegetarians are cheese, milk, and milk products, such as yogurt; eggs; nuts (such as almonds, cashew nuts, hazelnuts, Brazil nuts, walnuts, pine nuts, pecan nuts and peanuts); seeds (such as sunflower seeds, sesame seeds and pumpkin seeds); pulses (meaning all kinds of dried peas, beans and lentils, and products made from them, including tofu and hummus). Grains and products made from them (such as wholemeal bread, oatmeal, muesli, brown rice and pasta) are also a useful source of protein.

Although some of the vegetarian protein foods – nuts, grains and pulses – are lower in protein than meat and fish, getting enough protein on a vegetarian diet isn't usually a problem. In fact our protein requirement is very small, and a meat and fish diet actually supplies much more than we need. This excessive protein intake is not particularly healthy, and can lead to a loss of calcium (see page 247).

Sometimes people wonder whether non-animal protein is of the right quality, or whether it's necessary to balance vegetarian proteins carefully in order to get sufficient nutrients. It is true that by eating certain vegetable proteins together – beans and grains, for instance, as in baked beans on toast – your body can use more of the protein than if you ate them separately. But even so, in a normal diet, you do *not* have to eat any particular combinations in order to get sufficient protein. Since many foods – including potatoes, vegetables and grains – contain some protein, you will in any case mix proteins in almost any normal, varied meal.

CARBOHYDRATES AND FIBRE

Carbohydrate is needed for energy, to keep our bodies active and to keep them warm. It is found in starchy foods (sometimes called 'complex carbohydrates'), such as all types of cereals, bread, flour, pasta, potatoes and pulses. These foods are a source both of protein and complex carbohydrate. Fibre, which consists of the cellulose, wood and gums found in fruits, vegetables and grains, is also essential to the healthy functioning of the digestive system. Many of the diseases of the civilised world, from varicose veins to cancer of the bowel, have been attributed to lack of dietary fibre. A vegetarian diet contains plentiful amounts of both complex carbohydrates and fibre. Indeed, this is one of the advantages of such a diet from the point of view of the slimmer. Complex carbohydrates give a feeling of fullness, whilst fibre is helpful because it makes you chew and thus limits the amount you can eat in a given time!

Refined sugars and all foods containing sugar (such as honey, jam and fresh and dried fruit) are also a source of carbohydrate. Sugar is not, however, a healthy food. It has been extracted from very fibrous foods – sugar beet and cane. If you were to eat these in their natural state, the fibre would make it impossible for you to eat too much – you simply wouldn't be able to chew for long enough! Then, as it passed through your gut, it would take time for the sugar to be drawn out of the fibre, so your body would absorb it gently. The trouble with refined sugar is that it is all too easy to eat a lot. This piles on the Calories, and also puts a strain on your system because it is drawn into your bloodstream too quickly.

FATS AND CHOLESTEROL

Fats are needed for energy and warmth, and also for the absorption of the fat-soluble vitamins, A, D, E and K.

Too little fat may cause deficiencies in these vitamins. Fats are found in nuts, seeds and also in avocado pears; in milk, cheese, cream and egg yolk; in vegetable oils, butter and margarine. They can be divided roughly into three groups, according to their chemical structure. These are saturated fats (such as butter and other animal fats), but also coconut oil and palm oil; monosaturated fats (such as olive oil); and polyunsaturated fats, which include most vegetable oils (such as sunflower oil, corn oil and soya oil), as well as margarines made from these.

Cholesterol is found in the cells of the human body and of every animal, but not in any fruits, grains or vegetables. It is needed for many important body processes, but the body can make all it needs. If we take in too much saturated fat, our body makes more cholesterol than it needs; and when we eat foods which contain cholesterol, this adds to the levels, too. The higher the levels of cholesterol in our bloodstream, the greater our chances of having a heart attack.

Most of us eat too much fat, with around 40 per cent of our day's Calories coming from fat when 10 to 20 per cent would be the ideal! We particularly need to cut down on sources of saturated fat. This is easier for vegetarians, since they do not eat one major source – meat. But it's important not to over-emphasise cheese and eggs because they do contain saturated fat. They need to be used along with pulses, tofu, vegetables and grains – which contain little or no fat – and nuts, most of which contain polyunsaturated fat although there are some which contain saturated fat, for instance, peanuts and coconuts.

Olive oil is thought by many to be the healthiest oil for general use and in particular for cooking. This is because it reduces both the risk of heart disease associated with eating saturated animal fats, and also the possibility of increased incidence of cancer, which may be linked to the consumption of polyunsaturated fats especially when they are heated in cooking or in the production of margarine.

MINERALS AND MINERAL SALTS

CALCIUM

Calcium is needed for the health of bones, skin and teeth and for the function of the heart. It's also involved in blood-clotting. The richest sources of calcium are milk, cheese and yogurt, also leafy green vegetables, especially broccoli, cabbage, dried figs, sesame seeds and sesame cream (tahini). It's not difficult for a vegetarian to obtain enough calcium from these sources. Vegetarians who are not eating much dairy produce, and vegans, who are not eating any, may appear to have a rather low calcium intake. However there is a delicate balance between the amount of protein we eat and the amount of calcium we retain. When we eat more protein than we need, our kidneys have to work harder than usual to get rid of the excess. In doing this they draw on our supply of calcium. This calcium is then excreted, along with the excess protein. So eating too much protein can deplete our calcium supplies.

In a vegetarian diet, and particularly in a vegan diet, the protein levels are healthily low, which means that calcium is not wasted, and so less is needed. This is also why drinking extra milk or eating more cheese does not boost our calcium levels significantly, because these foods also push up our protein levels, and, in getting rid of the extra protein, we lose the calcium.

It is interesting to note that non-animal foods which contain useful amounts of calcium also contain iron — green vegetables, sesame seeds, pulses and dried fruit, for instance — whereas animal foods contain either one or the other. Milk and cheese are high in calcium but lack iron, while meat and eggs are rich in iron but lack calcium. Getting these minerals can be simpler on a well-balanced vegetarian diet.

IODINE

We need iodine for the proper functioning of the thyroid gland. This mineral is mainly found in fish and seafoods, including seaweeds. A good way for vegetarians and vegans to make sure they are getting enough of this vitamin is to use an iodised salt and to use agar agar or gelozone — vegetarian gelatines, made from seaweed — for making jellies. Kelp tablets, made from seaweed, are available from healthfood shops. They are a good supplement for anyone to take, because the iodine they contain helps protect against the destructive effects of radioactivity in the air.

IRON

Iron is needed for making blood and for carrying oxygen in the blood; lack of iron can cause anaemia. The best vegetarian sources of iron are pulses, wholegrain cereals (especially wholewheat bread, and millet, which contains the most iron of the grains); nuts and seeds; dark green vegetables; and dried fruits, especially dried peaches and apricots. Brewer's yeast, molasses (or black treacle), wheatgerm and egg yolk are also concentrated sources of iron. A vegetarian or vegan diet, planned along the lines suggested in this book, will meet the recommended iron levels. Such a diet will contain several slices of whole-wheat bread; a serving of pulses, sprouted pulses or nuts; a couple of servings of cereals such as muesli; rice or pasta, or a large jacket potato; a little dried fruit; and a serving of dark green leafy vegetables, plus other fruit and vegetables during the day.

MAGNESIUM

Magnesium, like phosphorus, is needed for healthy teeth and bones; it is also used in the process of drawing energy from carbohydrates. Almonds, Brazil nuts, peanuts and wheatgerm are all good sources of magnesium; also soya products (such as soya milk and tofu); and oats and millet. Leafy green vegetables, and fresh and dried fruit also contribute to your intake. Although it is not damaged by heat, magnesium is soluble, so you may lose some if you throw away the water used to cook vegetables. Use the water to make soups or sauces; or steam, bake or stir-fry vegetables instead.

MANGANESE

Manganese is another very important trace element which is used in the work of enzymes. It is found in wholewheat bread, wheatgerm, almonds, Brazil nuts, cashew nuts, peanuts and walnuts, as well as brewer's yeast, dried figs, dates, peaches and apricots. Fresh fruits and vegetables also supply some manganese. A vegetarian or vegan diet should not be short of this mineral.

PHOSPHORUS

This is needed, along with calcium, for healthy teeth and bones. Many foods contain phosphorus – nuts, fruits, vegetables, milk, eggs and cereals – so there is no problem in getting enough phosphorus on either a vegetarian or a vegan diet.

POTASSIUM AND SODIUM

Potassium and sodium are used together in the body to control the balance of fluids throughout the tissues and organs. The ratio of sodium to potassium is higher in the blood plasma and fluids, while in the muscles, organs and soft tissues of the body, potassium predominates. The better these proportions are maintained, the better our health is likely to be.

Sodium and potassium both occur in a very wide range of foods; however, in addition to this, we add sodium to our diet in the form of salt. Many manufactured goods, ranging from canned vegetables to breakfast cereals, contain high levels of sodium. So most people have too much sodium and too little potassium, which can cause a feeling of tiredness, since potassium is used in the process of carrying oxygen to the cells. A vegetarian or vegan diet, however, usually contains plenty of fresh fruit and vegetables, as well as wholegrains, wheatgerm and pulses, all of which are particularly rich sources of potassium, and thus help to redress the balance.

ZINC

Zinc is a mineral salt which is needed for bones and enzymes. A deficiency can cause skin problems such as eczema and acne, and may manifest as white flecks on the fingernails. The 'slimmers' diseases', anorexia and bulimia nervosa, have been linked with a shortage of zinc, although this is unlikely on a good diet. Zinc is found in wheatgerm, brewer's yeast, wholewheat bread and other grains; nuts and seeds, especially pumpkin seeds; pulses, cooked or sprouted; also green leafy vegetables, especially spinach; and sweetcorn, peas, mushrooms, fresh asparagus and mango. In addition, cheese, milk and yogurt can supply useful amounts for vegetarians. Vegans would be wise to use a good-quality soya milk which contains zinc, and include regular daily servings of the non-dairy foods mentioned above.

VITAMINS

VITAMIN A

Vitamin A is needed for the mucous membranes of the body, as well as healthy growth, resistance to infection and the functioning of the eyes. A lack of this vitamin increases the risk of bronchitis and also of infections in the throat, eyes and skin. Vitamin A is found in butter, eggs, cheese and fortified margarines, fortified skimmed milk and fortified evaporated milk. The body can make vitamin A from a substance called beta-carotene which is found in carrots, apricots and dark green leafy vegetables, and these are excellent sources of vitamin A. In addition, beta-carotene is thought to protect the body from some forms of cancer. A balanced vegetarian or vegan diet is usually rich in vitamin A.

B VITAMINS

There are thirteen B vitamins and these are grouped together because they're interdependent and (apart from

B12, see below) tend to occur in the same foods. They are needed for many bodily functions, ranging from the division of cells and the making of blood, to digestion, the proper functioning of the brain and resistance to infection. A deficiency may cause poor appetite, sores at the corners of the mouth and mouth ulcers. Lack of B vitamins may also result in irritability, depression, skin and scalp irritation, and a form of anaemia, and may contribute to heart disease and diabetes.

Good sources of B vitamins are: brewer's yeast, yeast extract, wheatgerm, fortified breakfast cereals, almonds, Brazil nuts, cashew nuts, hazelnuts, walnuts, sunflower seeds, sesame seeds, pumpkin seeds, peanuts (raw and roasted, but raw ones contain more thiamine), oatmeal, millet, brown rice, wholewheat bread, pulses, avocado pears, dark green leafy vegetables, dried fruits, milk, yogurt and cheese, mushrooms, bananas, oranges and pineapples. Some of the B vitamins are soluble and some are sensitive to heat, so, if you want to get the maximum amount, eat foods raw, steamed or stir-fried. Or if you do cook vegetables in water, save the water and use it in soups and sauces.

VITAMIN B12

Vitamin B12 is needed for similar functions to the other B vitamins, and in addition, for bone marrow formation. Lack of B12 can cause pernicious anaemia. B12 is found in meat and animal products, including dairy produce. It is almost entirely absent from plants, although some breakfast cereals, yeast extracts and soya milks are fortified with B12. Vegetarians can usually get enough of this vitamin, as can vegans, if they choose products which are fortified with B12. But taking B12 tablets may be advisable, to be on the safe side.

VITAMIN C

We need vitamin C for the absorption of iron, for tissue growth and repair, and for resistance to infection. Lack of this vitamin can cause anaemia and predisposition to infections. Vitamin C is present in many fresh fruits and vegetables; it is lost through contact with high temperatures, water and air, although cooked vegetables and potatoes contain useful amounts. A normal vegetarian or vegan diet, with its rich fruit and vegetable content, is unlikely to be lacking in this vitamin.

VITAMIN D

We need vitamin D in order to use calcium efficiently. This vitamin is present naturally in few foods, although some foods are fortified with vitamin D, notably margarine. Some types of bread and breakfast cereals, evaporated milk, some skimmed and soya milks are also fortified with this vitamin (read the labels to check). Apart from this, vegetarian sources of vitamin D are eggs, butter, fresh milk, cheese, yogurt and cottage cheese. Vitamin D is also formed by the action of sunlight on the skin, although people with dark skins cannot absorb vitamin D efficiently this way.

VITAMIN E

Vitamin E is needed for strong muscles and the functioning of the heart; it may increase fertility, and help prevent high blood pressure, atherosclerosis (hardening of the arteries) and some forms of cancer. It is also said to increase the body's ability to heal itself. Vitamin E is found in wheatgerm, nuts and seeds, wholegrains and products made from them. Eggs, butter and cheese are quite good sources, as are fruits. A vegetarian or vegan diet is not likely to be short of this vitamin.

VITAMIN K

Vitamin K is needed for blood clotting; it can be made by the bacteria in our intestines, and is also found in leafy green vegetables, tomatoes, soya bean oil, egg yolks and seaweed. A daily serving of leafy green vegetables will give you an adequate amount of this vitamin.

THE BEST SOURCES OF NUTRIENTS

You will have noticed that some foods crop up time and again in this section, because they are particularly good, concentrated sources of many nutrients. These are wheat-germ, sunflower, pumpkin and sesame seeds, brewer's yeast and yeast extracts, and dark green leafy vegetables. For maximum health and vitality, you should include these in your diet as often as possible. You probably won't need to take extra vitamin tablets, with the possible exception of vitamin B12 if you're vegan or a vegetarian eating very little dairy produce. A vegetarian or vegan diet planned along the lines suggested in this book will give you all the nutrients you need whilst helping you to lose weight.

Part 5
You Are More Than Your Physical Body

HOW ARE YOU FEELING?

In this section, we are going to look more closely at some of the mental and emotional factors which affect your ability to lose weight, and consider how you can get your body, senses, mind and emotions working together to create the body you have always wanted.

These four aspects of our being – our body, our senses, our emotions and our minds – need to be harmonised and made whole. If we ignore any one aspect, or pay it too much attention, we can get out of balance. Lack of harmony in our minds and emotions manifests as disease (including excess weight) in our physical bodies. As we attain a feeling of balance and harmony within ourselves, this shows as glowing health and vitality in our bodies.

Many of us go through most of our lives being out of touch with our feelings. We learn, often at an early age, that feelings are associated with pain. So, instead of expressing or acting on these feelings, we close off from them; or we rationalise our emotions, telling ourselves 'It doesn't really matter' or 'I don't really care', when really it does, and we do. We stifle these feelings, often being hardly aware of what we are doing, and frequently over-eating or drinking to compensate.

Usually when you ask someone how they are feeling, they will give a response from their head. The head is a great interpreter and wants to control everything, but it is not actually the part of us which experiences the feelings, senses and emotions. If you want to know what is really going on, you have to get in touch with the feeling directly, not just think about it. This is important because, to a very large degree, our bodies are the result of our thoughts and emotions. Everything is the result of energy in some form or other. The atoms and molecules of our bodies are energy. Every thought we have, every feeling, every sensation, is a result of a flow of energy. If we allow the energy to flow naturally and without hind-rance we can get in touch with a most exciting, dynamic aspect of our being.

But usually we learn at a very early age that this flow of energy needs to be curbed because it brings pain either to ourselves or to others. The truly open, loving heart is also very vulnerable, and when the flow of love is rejected and is turned back on itself we suffer pain. Instead of allowing energy to flow freely through us, we block it off and shut down to the level at which we feel comfortable. The energy then stays in the body and is stored there.

Most of us are conditioned, from childhood, to believe it is not possible to have what we want, or to put our wishes on one side, so we get out of touch with what we really do want to do. We hold on to our feelings, suppress them and put on weight, and in addition, we get a feeling of 'deadness'. Suppressed emotion helps to create the shape of our bodies. So we must look very carefully at the way we are blocking the flow of energy within our bodies.

Many people find that when they begin to notice their

feelings, and to express them, not only does the weight drop off, but they also find an 'aliveness' and enthusiasm for life which they never dreamt was possible. This is because it takes energy to hold back emotion. Once you accept and express the emotions, that energy is available for you to use in much more creative and productive ways. So what can you do about it?

Firstly you need to become aware of what you are really feeling, not what you *think* you are feeling, but what you are really feeling in your body, your 'gut reaction'. And then you need to know how to express these feelings effectively and appropriately; how to release anger safely, and how to communicate your needs and wishes to others.

So, start noticing how you are feeling. How are you feeling at this moment, for instance? Tense? Tired? Stressed? Relaxed? Keep monitoring the feelings in your body, your reactions to life. Do you really want to do what you are doing? What would you like to do? What is stopping you from doing that, or communicating that? What makes you feel excited and enthusiastic? What gives you a dead, dull feeling? The more you notice how you are feeling, the easier it becomes. You get in touch with what you really want, instead of what you think you ought to want. As you trust this 'gut feeling' and have the courage to follow it, you begin to come alive! New people and situations will come into your life and there will be a general feeling of vitality. This is because you are connecting with the real you. You are trusting your own instinct – or your intuition, or your 'higher self', as some people call it – and letting it flow through you.

Often all we need to do is to become aware of these feelings. They can guide us to lead our lives in a harmonious way. There are many times, however, when we need to communicate to others how we feel. For some of us, the process gets blocked at this point. We know how we feel, but we cannot get it across to others.

COMMUNICATING

The most important thing to remember when you are communicating with others is simply to say how you feel. Say it directly to the person concerned, preferably not by phone or letter, and certainly not through another person. Keep the message simple and clear. Don't make judgements about what the other person is doing to you, or assumptions about what they'll think or how they'll react. For instance, don't say 'You'll probably think I'm stupid saying this, but . . .' or 'I'm sure you won't agree with me, but . . .' or 'You probably won't like hearing this, but . . .' These statements may or may not be true but they are pre-judging the situation. So just keep to a straightforward statement of the one thing that you do know to be true: how you are feeling. Begin with phrases like: 'I think . . .', 'I like . . .', 'I don't like . . .', 'I appreciate . . .', 'I feel . . .', 'I believe . . .', 'I value . . .', 'I disagree with . . .'

It is much more powerful, honest and effective to own the statement by saying what *you* feel, rather than what people in general might think. When you begin your sentences with 'I . . .', other people will sense the integrity and authenticity of what you are saying and are likely to respond positively to it.

Always repeat what you have said if you feel you are not being understood. Again it is most effective if *you* take the responsibility. 'I feel I am being misunderstood', not 'You don't understand me'. In the same way, if you are feeling confused, or you are not able to say what you are feeling clearly, say so. Keep to the unarguable facts and avoid blaming or judging the other person. Speaking the truth simply, like this, is powerful and effective because it 'rings true' to the other person. They, in turn, are then more likely to be open and honest with you.

Of course communication is a two-way affair and, although it feels good to say how you are feeling, you still need to get a response from the other person. So when you have said what you need to say, encourage the other person to say how they are feeling. Not what they are *thinking* but how they are feeling *right now*.

When the other person talks, it is important to listen quietly without interrupting. Don't blame, judge, criticise, defend or take offence. They are simply communicating their feelings; there is no need for you to take it personally or to offer an opinion. If you feel an emotion, you can say so, but don't blame. Say 'I feel hurt/angry/upset by what you have said', not 'You have hurt/upset me/made me angry'. They haven't done that to you. They have simply told you how they are feeling. You do not have to be hurt, angry or upset by what they say. No one can make you feel these things. You are 100 per cent responsible for your feelings. Once you realise the full impact of this, you become master of your life and not the victim of other people and circumstances.

ASKING FOR WHAT YOU WANT

In the same way, when you want someone to do something for you, say it in a direct way: 'Please will you make me a cup of tea', rather than 'I don't suppose you'd like to make a cup of tea, would you?' or 'A cup of tea would be nice'. It's true that the other person can say 'No' and you may feel rejected, or not (remember, that is up to you). But that way the whole communication has been clean.

You have each said what you feel and there has been no manipulation.

Tell the person that you would like their help. Use direct words such as: 'I need . . .', 'I want . . .', 'I desire . . .', 'I would really appreciate your help/support . . .' If you can, add a reason, to make the situation clearer. For instance: '*I need* you to go over the household accounts with me *because* I feel worried when I do not know how much money we have.' This is much cleaner and more effective than using statements such as: 'You know I always hate it when . . .', 'You know I don't like . . .', or 'You know I'm frightened of . . .' When I hear or read statements like this, I get a sinking feeling. They are statements which make assumptions and have a sense of blame. They lead to confused communication. It's best not to use them, and if other people say them to you, encourage them to communicate clearly too by asking them what they are really feeling and what they really want.

SAYING 'NO'

It's very important to be able to say 'No' if you don't want to do something, but many people find this very difficult. Again, be aware of how you feel. Do you really want to do whatever it is? If it feels wrong to you, say 'No'. The key lies in saying how you feel and saying it directly: 'No, I don't want to . . .', 'No, I have decided not to . . .', 'No, I don't feel comfortable with that . . .', rather than 'I'd like to, but . . .', or 'Denis won't let me . . .'

Then, though it isn't necessary, it helps to give a reason: 'No, I don't want to come to the meeting *because* I have too many other commitments at the moment. But thank you for asking me.' The final 'thank you' tells the other person that you are not rejecting them, only their request.

Once you know that you have the power to decide whether something feels right to you or not, and that you can say 'No' comfortably, it gives you a feeling of being in control.

DEALING WITH ANGER

Perhaps the emotion that you are feeling is not one which you can communicate easily. Maybe you feel angry with someone or some situation in your life. Many of us have been conditioned to believe that it is 'wrong' to feel emotions, particularly anger. But anger is only an energy like any other. It is not the energy which is 'wrong' but the ways in which people sometimes express it. For instance, you may bottle the anger up, and then, when you can contain it no longer, you 'blow your top'. When this happens, often the event which seems to make us angry or upset – the 'last straw' – is not the real cause of our upset at all.

When you feel angry about something, ask yourself if that is what you are really upset about, or is it something else? Work the feeling back in your mind, step by step, until you get to the deepest emotion, and communicate this. Do this as near the time when you are feeling it as you can. Bottling up feelings is like storing up fat; the two are closely related, and both equally hard to shift!

It's important to recognise that this anger is your responsibility. Yes, the other person, or the situation, may have acted as a trigger, but what you feel is your anger and it needs to be let out safely and appropriately. That does not mean that you have to scream at the person concerned. It is perfectly all right to tell them 'I am feeling very angry', but don't say 'You are making me feel very angry'. They are not. You are responsible for your own feelings, your own anger. So let it out, but do so safely.

When you think to yourself 'I feel I could scream', go outside or get into your car and do so. Really scream and shout! It may seem ridiculous, but you will feel so much better afterwards. Or have an 'anger release': take a rolling pin or a tennis racquet, kneel down and really thump a pillow or a mattress until you can thump it no more! Swing at it from your hips, throwing your whole body into the action. This feels really good. You may be amazed at how much power and energy you have. Once it is flowing, this power and energy can be used positively to do the things you want to do, instead of being battened down inside, causing you to over-eat and put on weight.

Once you are aware of this anger, and accept that it is a vital life-force, you can learn to release it in safe ways, and use the energy positively. Feel the anger – or energy – within you and let it spur you on. Let it invigorate you and help you to get slim, to do all the things you want to do.

LEARNING TO LOVE YOURSELF

Many people over-eat because they feel unhappy about themselves and their lives. They say they feel unloved, but, deep down, the problem is that they do not like themselves. 'I'm not good enough' is a belief which many of us pick up as young children. Our first view of ourselves is created by what adults tell us when we are very young; most of our conditioning takes place before we are three years old.

These beliefs about ourselves remain with us for the rest of our lives, unless we do something about them. And because little children often get the idea that they are inferior, unimportant, silly or a nuisance, it is natural for most of us to lack confidence. How often do you use expressions such as 'I won't keep you a moment', 'It's only me', 'It doesn't really matter', or 'I don't mind . . .'? We feel that we are unimportant and have no right to get our needs met, when really we have just as much right to be here as anyone else.

Because we lack confidence in ourselves, and secretly fear that we are not lovable, we look to other people to praise and love us. But no matter how much praise and love we get, if the fears are there, they will surface sooner or later. When we depend on other people to give us confidence and love – and happiness – we make ourselves very insecure. We are giving away our own power. We need to learn to love and nurture ourselves, in order to be truly secure and free.

Once you truly love yourself, your relationships work better because you free yourself from the fear of failure and from jealousy and insecurity. You can give more, without demanding anything in return. You have the confidence to know that if a relationship ends, you can be happy on your own, or you can have another relationship which is equally good and fulfilling.

So how do you achieve this state of loving yourself? First of all, notice whenever you criticise yourself or put yourself down. How often during the day do you think 'I can't do that'. 'I'm not clever enough', 'Silly me', 'I should/shouldn't have done that'? From now on:

• Resolve to banish 'should' and 'ought' from your vocabulary.
• Every time you catch yourself thinking something critical or negative about yourself, immediately replace it with these words: 'I love and approve of myself. I love and

approve of myself. I love and approve of myself . . .' Say it often – you can't say it too often.

● Stop punishing yourself with thoughts of past mistakes or failures. Think of the things you did *right*. Think of your positive qualities; all your lovable characteristics.

● Start treating yourself with love. Treat yourself as you would treat someone very dear to you. Listen to your feelings, as described on page 257. Create pleasant conditions for yourself; buy yourself some flowers, a book, a cassette or something new to wear . . .

● Listen to your body and its needs. Don't drive it too hard. Wear comfortable clothes. Don't force your feet into shoes that pinch. Allow yourself to relax and sleep when you want to; or, if your body is yearning for exercise, make time for this.

As you start to love yourself, you will notice some changes. At first, it may seem as if what you are doing is having a negative effect. One or two things may happen to knock your confidence or make you feel unloved or inferior. This is good! Don't let it disturb you, this phase will quickly pass. It means that what you are doing is stirring up negative beliefs which are coming out. Just keep on saying 'I love and approve of myself' and treating yourself well, and very soon you will start getting positive feedback. If you feel love for yourself, the world, which is your mirror, will reflect love back to you. People will begin to treat you with more love and respect; *they* will start commenting on all your good and lovable points.

You will soon feel happier, more contented and more vital, and you will look more beautiful. Having a beautiful body starts with loving yourself, loving your body and allowing energy to flow through you. You will also find that you are more loving towards those around you.

Loving and accepting others requires us to love and accept ourselves.

LETTING GO OF NEGATIVE EMOTIONS

Hanging on to negative emotions (fears, or resentment about what other people did to us in the past, or guilt about what we did or didn't do to them) often goes hand in hand with hanging on to fat in our bodies. As we let go of these negative emotions, we let go of the weight. The hard lump of hurt and pain melts, and we get a sense of freedom, space and love.

When you think about it, it is ridiculous to allow your thoughts and memories of the past – or your fears about the future – to spoil the present moment. The fact that you did something in the past that you regret, or that someone did something to you which caused you pain, need not spoil what's happening now. All you are experiencing is your memory of the past. Your memory is hurting *you*, no one else. It is over and done with. Let the past go, and enjoy the reality of the present moment. You can choose to be at peace in your thoughts or to be worried and fearful. This does not mean suppressing negative feelings. It means acknowledging them and expressing them if you want to do so. But it also means not allowing them to shatter your inner peace; to realise that you can be at peace, and feel love, no matter what is happening.

Letting go of negative emotions sounds easy, but for many of us it can be quite difficult. Loving yourself, as described above, will help, as will replacing negative thoughts of any kind immediately with 'I love and approve of myself' (see Affirmations, page 278). But if you are troubled by thoughts of guilt or resentment, you will need to forgive either yourself or another. Forgiveness dissolves that hard lump within. But how do you forgive? In her book, *You Can Heal Your Life* (page 303), Louise Hay suggests an exercise where you imagine you are sitting in a darkened theatre looking at a small stage. Then you see the person you want to forgive come on to that stage and you see good things happening to them. You see them smiling and happy. Say 'I forgive you ——; I forgive you for not being the way I wanted you to be. I forgive you and I set you free.' Next, see yourself on the stage, and visualise good things happening to you. Louise Hay suggests that you do this exercise every day for a month, and says that during that time you may see different people on the stage as the process of forgiveness takes place in your life. If thoughts of resentment come into your mind, you can say the forgiveness words again in your head each time.

What if you really can't forgive? In her book, *Think Slim, Be Slim* (page 303), Elsye Birkinshaw suggests that you visualise the person you want to forgive on a stage as described above, and then say: 'God, please forgive this person in my name. I cannot do it. I know *you* can forgive him and I will thus be released.' If you do not feel happy with the word 'God', which has many confusing associations, you may prefer to use another, such as 'Source', 'Higher Power Within Me', 'Universal Self' or 'Spirit'. The name is not important; what is important is your desire for forgiveness to take place, and your act of surrender.

REPROGRAMMING OUR BELIEFS

Our minds have an extraordinary power over our bodies, our behaviour and even the events that occur in our lives. We 'program' our minds with negative thoughts about ourselves, such as 'I can't stick to a diet', 'Nothing works for me', and so on. These are often beliefs which we picked up when we were very little. How often can you hear the voice of a parent or teacher when you think 'Well, you can't have everything you want, you know', or 'You must eat up everything on your plate'? These almost unconscious thoughts can literally run our lives without our realising it.

You may not be getting slim because, deep down inside, you believe that you will fail, or that you can't cope with the pressures of being successful. You may have a little inner voice which says 'You always fail' or 'You can never stick to anything', or 'Success is painful', perhaps an idea you picked up when really young, and it has stuck at an unconscious level. Think back to your childhood and see if anything comes to mind, perhaps in connection with your parents, and their apparent success or failure. What may be happening now is that whenever you almost succeed at slimming (or anything else) something inside you makes you mess things up. Perhaps this is because you believe you always fail, or that success is associated with pain and stress in some way.

If we can affect our lives by our thoughts, think what you are doing to yourself and your life when you continually think negative thoughts! Yet a thought can be changed. And a change of thought can lead to a complete change in your life.

You can make these changes in two ways: by creative visualisation, 'seeing' yourself as slim, doing what you want to do in your life; and by affirmations, saying over and over to yourself a positive thought instead of a negative one. (The sentence 'I love and approve of myself' which I gave in the section on Loving Yourself (page 262) is an example of an affirmation.) It is a good idea to say an affirmation whenever a negative thought comes into your mind. As well as this, an excellent time for doing both affirmations and creative visualisation is after relaxation or meditation. For more about all these helpful techniques, see the relevant sections on Affirmations (page 278), Visualisation (page 275), Relaxation (page 270), and Meditation (page 271).

Sometimes we hang on to our weight because, for some reason, we need an excuse for not doing something in our lives. We keep putting off taking action, saying that we can't do it until we're slim. If you think this may be the case, ask yourself whether you *really* want to do it, and what, apart from not being, in your eyes, slim enough, is preventing you? Perhaps it's fear of failure, change, or commitment? There are always fears about making changes or starting something new. Don't let memories of the past, or other people's opinions, put you off. If there is something you really want to do, have the courage of your convictions and do it. Think of the things you are waiting for. What do you have to do to make them happen? Make three columns on a sheet of paper. On the left-hand side, write the things you want to do. Beside each, in the next column, write the reasons why you think you can't do them. Then, in the right-hand column, write down the ways in which you can overcome each of these obstacles. You may find the difficulties are more imaginary than real. Difficulties can be overcome if you want to overcome them!

George Bernard Shaw said: 'People are always blaming their circumstances for what they are. I don't believe in circumstances. The people who get on in this world are the people who get up and look for circumstances they want, and, if they can't find them, make them.'

The hardest part of a task is starting it, taking the

initiative. But once you begin, once you take the first step, the energy starts flowing through you. You take control; you become powerful and effective.

'Act boldly, and unseen forces will come to your aid. Go confidently in the direction of your dreams, act as though it were impossible to fail. Dare to lead the life you have dreamed for yourself; go forward and make those dreams come true.'

RELAXATION AND MEDITATION

As well as the four aspects of our being – body, senses, mind and emotions – which I have already described, there is another, which is sometimes called our spirit, Self, higher self, or transpersonal self. This is the aspect of ourselves which manifests sometimes at times of crisis; in deep prayer and meditation; in mystical experiences. Those who have touched it say they experienced great strength, comfort, peace and healing. I personally find it very comforting to remember that this aspect of my being is there, waiting to guide, inspire and heal me.

Relaxation, meditation, creative visualisation and affirmations are all tools which can help us to become aware of this power. They are also valid at a mental and physical level because they help to release stress. When we are stressed – which happens to us all during the normal course of a day – we tense up our muscles. One of the responses to tension is to over-eat, drink or smoke. When we practise relaxation, we release the tension and thus ease the stress. This makes us less likely to want to comfort ourselves through food, drink or smoking.

Relaxation gives us a feeling of harmony and well-being. It helps to put us in touch with our bodies and their true needs, and it puts us in contact with our unconscious. We are thus more open to the wisdom which can flow from the Self; we are also more responsive to positive imaging, suggestion and affirmations (see page 278). Relaxation can be done at any time of the day or night; and it can be done several times a day if you wish. I find that if I can't sleep in the night, running through the sequence below usually does the trick, and often I don't manage to get right to the end of it. There are numerous methods of relaxation. Here is one of the simplest and most effective, but you might like to get your doctor's agreement first if you are worried by high blood pressure. In this case, do the meditation instead, which, when practised daily, has been shown to reduce high blood pressure.

RELAXATION

Here is a simple but effective technique for relaxation. A relaxation such as this takes 15–30 minutes and is as refreshing as a sleep. It is a great way to release tension, to refresh yourself and also to get in touch with your inner sense of peace.

● First, make yourself comfortable. It is best to lie down on a bed or on the floor, with a pillow or cushion under your head and a blanket over you. It's important to be warm enough.
● Lie on your back with your hands loosely at your sides. Close your eyes.
● The idea is to tense and then relax each part of your body in turn. Start with your toes; curl them up as hard as you can, hold for a few seconds, then relax.
● Tense your feet and lower legs; then relax.

270

• Tighten your leg muscles from your hip bone to your feet; hold, then relax.
• Squeeze your buttocks together; relax.
• Pull in your stomach muscles; relax.
• Tighten your ribs and chest; relax.
• Clench your fists and tense your arms; let go.
• Lift and hunch your shoulders; then relax.
• Tense and lift your neck; then let your head flop.
• Clench your jaw and press your tongue against your teeth; relax.
• Screw up your eyes and face; relax.
• Imagine your scalp relaxed. Now imagine a wave of warmth and relaxation wash over you from head to toe. Say to yourself: 'I am deeply relaxed from head to toe.'

You should be feeling very warm and relaxed. If you want to do creative visualisation and/or affirmations, do them now. Your mind will be at its most receptive. Then, when you are ready, open your eyes and get up slowly.

MEDITATION

Meditation is a process in which we sit absolutely still, with our minds relaxed but aware and our bodies peaceful. This enables us to get in touch with parts of our being which are normally unheard or unnoticed because we are so busy doing and thinking things in our everyday lives. These more subtle parts speak very softly and gently at first, but as you get in touch with them they become stronger. They will bring peace and healing. You will find that you look forward to your meditation times each day and that your life will seem strangely empty if you skip them; as if something is missing.

In his book, *How to Meditate* (page 304), Lawrence LeShan says:

'We meditate to find, to recover, to come back to something of ourselves we once dimly and unknowingly had and have lost without knowing what it was or where or when we lost it. We may call it access to more of our human potential or being closer to ourselves and reality, or to more of our capacity for love and zest and enthusiasm, or our knowledge that we are a part of the universe and can never be alienated or separated from it, or our ability to see and function in reality more effectively.'

People who practise meditation regularly notice a marked sense of peace and also a greater feeling of 'aliveness'. Without the distractions of the mind or the body, we become aware of our essential unity. Again I quote from LeShan:

'The thrust, individuality and vibrancy of our perception of the individual person are heightened by our perception of the oneness we share with him as we both shade into the whole planet, all others and the total universe . . . If I *know* that you and I are both one, that we are not separated and that I am not only my brother's keeper but also my brother, I will treat you as I treat myself. Further, since I know that I am part of the total cosmos, of all Being, I will treat myself, and therefore you, as something precious.'

Through meditation, we also begin to pay attention to the *whole* of ourselves. We look at the 'bad' bits as well as the 'good' bits, but without judgement. So there is a feeling of ease, of being able to be truly ourselves without fear of criticism or condemnation.

There are many different types of meditation. Here is a good one to begin with. You can practise twice a day for at least 10 but not more than 20 minutes; or you can do the meditation in the morning and the relaxation described above in the evening.

PREPARATION FOR MEDITATION

You need to find somewhere to meditate where you will not be disturbed, although once you get used to the technique, it is surprising how little outer conditions intrude. (I have had some excellent meditations on trains and planes.) It is a good idea to put any animals into another room; they may be attracted by the energy which they sense when you are meditating and may disturb you. Take the phone off the hook. Have a watch or clock within sight, or set a timer, but avoid clocks with a loud 'tick' or timers with strident alarms. (Put the timer under a pillow if necessary to muffle it.) Sit comfortably, either on a straight-backed chair or, if you can do so, cross-legged or in a lotus or half-lotus position on a good cushion on the floor, provided you find this easy and comfortable. Do *not* do this if there is any sense of forcing or strain on your knees. Have your hands on your lap, left hand cupped within the right. Check that your spine is straight; loosen any tight clothing. Close your eyes.

WATCHING YOUR BREATH MEDITATION

Keeping your eyes closed, take a few deep breaths, and as you breathe out, feel that you are letting go, perhaps with a sigh.

Now put your attention on your breath. Watch your breath as if you were an observer. Don't make any effort to breathe. Just wait for the breath and trust that it will enter. Don't try to change the pace of your breathing at all. Just watch it. Feel the breath rippling through you. There is nothing to do.

If you find that your attention wanders and other thoughts come into your mind, don't do anything until you get the thought 'I'm not watching my breathing'. Then, very gently, bring your attention back to your breathing. There should be nothing forced or strained about this process, just a gentle, easy, relaxed 'being'.

At the end of 20 minutes, slowly open your eyes and bring your attention back to the normal everyday world. Take some deep breaths, then gently get up.

OTHER TYPES OF MEDITATION

Once you are used to this meditation, there are variations which you might like to try. In one of these, you count your breaths as they come in. You count up to a given number – ten is the number often recommended – and then when you get to that number, you start again. When you lose track of the counting because of thoughts, simply start again at 'One'.

In another form of meditation, instead of counting, you repeat a word, or 'mantra' to yourself throughout your meditation. This is one of the most widely practised forms of meditation. The aim is to be aware of your word, just as in the breathing meditation you were aware only of your breath.

You can choose your own mantra. You may choose a phrase which is meaningful to you, such as 'God is Love' or 'I am love'; or you may choose two or three syllables which have no meaning but sound good to you. In her book, *Loving Relationships* (page 304), Sondra Ray suggests the mantra 'Om Namaha Shivai', which has many meanings, including 'Infinite Being, Infinite Intelligence and Infinite Manifestation'. She also suggests the mantra 'I am increasing my willingness to be loved', which she has found to be effective. LeShan suggests a practical, no-nonsense approach to finding a completely neutral mantra. He recommends you open a telephone book at random and put a finger down blindly. Take the first syllable of the name you hit. Then repeat the process. Link the two syllables and you have your mantra.

VISUALISATION AND AFFIRMATIONS

VISUALISATION

For creative visualisation, start in a comfortable relaxed state, such as you are in at the end of your relaxation or meditation, or when you first wake up in the morning. When we are in that drowsy state between sleeping and waking, our minds are not as active as usual, the critical, rational part is suppressed, and we are more responsive to new ideas and affirmations.

Imagine yourself in a place where you feel really comfortable. It may be a place you know from the past; it may be your home, or outdoors. Or it may be imaginary, perhaps a sunlit beach, under pine trees, in a quiet clearing in a wood, or by a lake or river. Picture the scene as clearly as you can. Be aware of the scents and sounds; feel the sun and gentle breeze on your face. Now picture yourself as you would like to be: slim, vital, supple, glowing with health. See yourself surrounded by your friends and loved ones; see their faces and feel their positive response to you. You may need several minutes or a shorter time to do this, whatever feels right to you. Enjoy the experience, have fun with it, make it what you really want. When you have finished, make an affirmation, such as 'I love and approve of myself'. Then end with the words: 'This or something better now manifests for me for the total benefit of all concerned.' This is important, because it allows for something even better than you had envisaged.

Don't worry if you can't picture the scene clearly (or at all). Just 'thinking' it as if you were day-dreaming is enough. Do what feels easy and natural and enjoyable to you. If negative thoughts come up, such as 'That couldn't possibly happen'; don't try to stop them. Just let them flow through your consciousness, and then go back to your visualisation. It is important never to resist negative thoughts, because this just gives them more power. They're only thoughts; let them be. They will pass.

These are the steps for creative visualisation:

• Set your goal – whatever you want to achieve in your life. In this case, we are concentrating on your perfect body, but creative visualisation can be used in any aspect of your life, such as your home, family life, relationships, your job or your health.

• Create a clear idea of what you want; see it exactly as you would like it to be, and see it in the present. Experience it as though you already have it. Include as many details as you can.

• Picture it often, during your relaxation and meditation periods, and also during the day, whenever you think of it. The more you think of it, the more you believe it and it becomes a part of your life.

• Continue to visualise your goal until you achieve it, or until it is no longer relevant. If you realise that you want to change your goal before you have reached it, that is perfectly OK. Goals may change and develop as we do; allow this to happen.

MAKING A PICTURE

It's very helpful to reinforce your creative visualisation with a picture of how you would like to be. Look through magazines and find a picture of someone with the sort of body you would like to have. Cut it out and stick it on a piece of paper or card. If you like you can even cut out their face and stick it on a photograph of your own. Add any other inspiring remarks or colourful pictures which you think may help to reinforce the image. For instance, you might draw a balloon coming out of the model's mouth with the words: 'Now I am my perfect weight and looking and feeling wonderful.' You might also like to include any affirmations such as 'I love and approve of myself.' Also write the words 'This or something better now manifests for me for the total benefit of all concerned', as explained above.

MAKING A NOTEBOOK

A creative visualisation notebook is fun to make and can be helpful because it reinforces your positive ideas. Get a large book with unlined pages. Write in this your goals and favourite affirmations; positive sayings which appeal to you; pictures of your goal – you can include in it a picture of your perfect figure, with your face on it, as described above. Write down a list of all the things you appreciate in your life and add to this list as you think of more things; all the things you like about yourself – again, add to this as you think of more things. This helps to reinforce your self-esteem, and the more this is strengthened, the happier you will be and the more you will have to give to others. You can also write down a list of treats you can give yourself. These can be small or large, but make some of them things that you can do every day, such as have a bubble bath, buy a new magazine, have 10 minutes of relaxation with your feet up, and so on. You can also include fantasies and creative ideas – these can be as wild or apparently unrealistic as you like. Jot them down anyway. By allowing your mind to contemplate them you are helping to unlock your creativity.

This notebook is a powerful tool in helping you to realise your goal. Just a few minutes spent on it each day, recording your progress and noting thoughts and ideas, will be worth much more time in terms of results. Have fun with this book; make it as colourful as you like. Enjoy it!

POSITIVE IMAGES AND AFFIRMATIONS AROUND THE HOUSE

These are inspiring and act as helpful reminders during the day. Write out your affirmation(s) and stick them in places where you will see them: on the fridge door, on your desk, by the mirror in the hall. Again, a picture of your perfect figure stuck to the fridge door can work wonders!

AFFIRMATIONS

An affirmation is a positive statement such as 'I love and approve of myself.' Here are some others you could try:

'I am at peace with my own feelings. I am safe where I am. I create my own security. I love and approve of myself.'

'I am now putting my life in order, preparing to accept all the good that is coming to me now.'

'I give thanks for all the good things that I have and all the good things to come.'

'I now release my entire past. It is complete and I am free.'

'I now resolve all negative, limiting beliefs. They have no power over me.'

'I now forgive and release everyone in my life. They are all free and I am free.'

'I now let go of all accumulated guilt, fears, resentment, disappointments and grudges. I am free and they are free.'

'All barriers to my full self-expression and enjoyment of life are now dissolved.'

'The world is a beautiful place to be.'

'The universe always provides.'

'I accept myself completely here and now.'

'I love myself completely as I am, and I'm getting better all the time.'

'I accept all my feelings as part of myself.'

'It's good to express my feelings. I now give myself permission to express my feelings.'

'It's OK for me to enjoy myself and have fun.'

'I am now deeply relaxed and centred.'

'I now feel deep inner peace and serenity.'

'The light within me is creating miracles in my body and mind, here and now.'

'I am beautiful and lovable.'

'I am kind and loving, and I have a great deal to share with others.'

'I am talented, intelligent and creative.'

'I am growing more and more attractive every day.'

'I deserve the very best in life.'

'I have a lot to offer and everyone recognises it.'

'I love the world and the world loves me.'

'I am willing to be happy and successful.'

'I accept my good, which is flowing to me here and now.'

'I deserve the best and the best is coming to me here and now.'

'I love and accept myself completely as I am.'

'I express myself freely, fully and easily.'

'I am a powerful, loving and creative being.'

'I am a lovable and loving person.'

'I am whole in myself.'

'I can relax and let go.'

'I can go with the flow.'

'I have all the love I need within my own heart.'

'I always have everything I need to enjoy my here and now.'

HOW TO MAKE AFFIRMATIONS

• Always phrase affirmations in the present tense – 'I am

slim and beautiful' – the unconscious mind does not understand affirmations in the future tense.

• Remember when making an affirmation that you are not trying to undo the past or change the present. You need to start by accepting the present and loving yourself (or the situation) as you are now, whilst at the same time creating yourself or your situation as you want it or them to be in the future. You are accepting what 'is' in your life but at the same time realising that every moment brings a new opportunity to create exactly what you desire.

• Always phrase affirmations in the most positive way you can. Avoid negative affirmations. For instance, don't say 'I am no longer overweight.' Say 'I am now slim and beautiful.'

• Keep affirmations as short and simple as you can. These are much easier to remember and more powerful in their effect.

• An affirmation should feel right. As you say it, it should feel freeing; you might get a sense of tension relaxing, an 'aaah' as you say it. If it doesn't feel right, change the words around until it does, or try another affirmation.

CALORIE AND COMPATIBILITY GUIDE TO BASIC FOODS

Calories are given in the first column. The second column, for the food-combining diet, shows whether the food is:

Protein or compatible with protein (P)
Carbohydrate or compatible with carbohydrate (C)
Neutral – compatible with both protein and carbohydrate (N)

Almonds		N,P
shelled, 25 g/1 oz	169	
sugared, each	15	
flaked, 15 ml tablespoon	35	
ground, 15 ml tablespoon	40	
whole, each	10	
Angelica		C
25 g/1 oz	90	
Apples		P
dried, 25 g/1 oz	71	
juice unsweetened, 25 g/1 oz	10	
apple, eating, each medium	50	
apple, eating, flesh, 25 g/1 oz	10	
apples, cooking, baked whole	80	
apples, cooking, flesh, 25 g/1 oz	10	
Apricots		P
fresh, each	5	
dried, 25 g/1 oz	54	
dried, each	15	
canned in juice, 25 g/1 oz	13	
canned in syrup, 25 g/1 oz	30	
Arrowroot		C
25 g/1 oz	100	
5 ml teaspoon	10	

Artichokes, globe   N
  globe, each   10
  artichoke hearts, 415 g/15 oz can   24
  canned, 25 g/1 oz   3
Artichokes, Jerusalem   C[1]
  boiled, 25 g/1 oz   5
Asparagus   N
  boiled or fresh, each   5
Aubergines   N
  raw, each, 200 g/7 oz   28
  raw, 25 g/1 oz   4
  sliced, fried, 25 g/1 oz   60
Avocado pears   N
  25 g/1 oz   63
  avocado pears, half   240
Baked beans   P
  25 g/1 oz   20
  225 g/8 oz can   160
Baking powder   N
  5 ml teaspoon   5
Bamboo shoots   N
  canned, 25 g/1 oz   5
Bananas   C
  small, each   55
  medium, each   80
  large, each   95
  fresh, flesh only, 25 g/1 oz   22
  dried, 25 g/1 oz   140

[1] Dr Hay always classified these as carbohydrate, but I think they should be considered neutral, since they contain 3.8% carbohydrate. Foods normally contain at least 22% carbohydrate to fall into this category.

Barley C
  pearl, dry, 25 g/1 oz 102
  pearl, 15 ml tablespoon 45
Beansprouts N
  raw, 25 g/1 oz 8
Beans P[2]
  aduki, dry, 25 g/1 oz 92
  aduki, cooked, 25 g/1 oz 40
  baked, 25 g/1 oz 20
  baked, no added sugar, 25 g/1 oz 16
  broad, boiled or fresh, 25 g/1 oz 12
  butterbeans, dry, 25 g/1 oz 75
  butterbeans, cooked or canned,
  25 g/1 oz 26
  cannellini, dry, 25 g/1 oz 75
  cannellini, cooked or canned,
  25 g/1 oz 26
  chickpeas, dry, 25 g/1 oz 78
  chickpeas, cooked or canned, 25 g/1 oz 26
  flageolet, dry, 25 g/1 oz 77
  flageolet, boiled, 25 g/1 oz 32
  French or runner, boiled, 25 g/1 oz 7
  lentils, dry, 25 g/1 oz 84
  lentils, cooked or canned, 25 g/1 oz 27
  mung, dry, 25 g/1 oz 92
  red kidney, dry, 25 g/1 oz 73
  red kidney, cooked or canned,
  25 g/1 oz 25
  soya beans, dry, 25 g/1 oz 108
  beans, sprouted, bean still attached, P
  25 g/1 oz 28

[2]For food-combining, best eaten just with other vegetables, not with other proteins.

Beer		C
300 ml/10 fl oz	100	
Beetroot		N
raw, 25 g/1 oz	8	
boiled, 25 g/1 oz	12	
Biscuits		C.
per average-size biscuit, approximate		
chocolate chip cookie	60	
chocolate finger	30	
crunchy bar, Jordan's	137	
digestive, large	70	
Blackberries		P
raw, 25 g/1 oz	8	
Blackcurrants		P
raw, 25 g/1 oz	8	
Blueberries		P
raw, 25 g/1 oz	8	
Brazil nuts		N,P
shelled, 25 g/1 oz	182	
each	20	
Bread		C
100% wholemeal, 25 g/1 oz	61	
malt, 25 g/1 oz	70	
white, 25 g/1 oz	66	
French, 25 g/1 oz	85	
white, dried crumbs, 25 g/1 oz	100	
bap, 42 g/1½ oz	130	
Chapati, one large, made with fat	95	
one large, made without fat	57	
crumpet, 42 g/1½ oz	75	
croissant, 65 g/2½ oz	280	
currant bun, 45 g/1¾ oz	150	
hot cross bun, 50 g/2 oz	180	
pitta, 65 g/2½ oz	205	

roll, 45 g/1¾ oz		145
scone, plain, 50 g/2 oz		160
Breadcrumbs		C
dried, 15 ml tablespoon		30
fresh, 15 ml tablespoon		8
Breakfast cereals		C
All-bran, 25 g/1 oz		88
bran, 25 g/1 oz		58
Bran flakes, 25 g/1 oz		85
cornflakes, 25 g/1 oz		100
Granola style cereals, 25 g/1 oz		135
Grapenuts, 25 g/1 oz		101
muesli, 25 g/1 oz		105
porridge oats, 25 g/1 oz		115
porridge, cooked with water and salt, 25 g/1 oz		12
puffed rice etc, 25 g/1 oz		100
Rice Krispies, 25 g/1 oz		100
Shredded Wheat, per biscuit		75
Weetabix, per biscuit		65
Broccoli		N
fresh or boiled, 25 g/1 oz		4
Brussels sprouts		N
raw, 25 g/1 oz		9
boiled, 25 g/1 oz		5
Bulgar wheat		C
25 g/1 oz		104
Butter		N
25 g/1 oz		225
Buttermilk		P
25 g/1 oz		12
Cabbage		N
raw, 25 g/1 oz		7
boiled, 25 g/1 oz		2

Cakes

chocolate sponge, iced and filled, 125 g/4 oz	330
rich fruit cake, with/without icing and marzipan 50 g/2 oz	200
chocolate eclair with real cream 75 g/3 oz	300
Danish pastry, 1 small	210
doughnut, jam	270

Carob   C

flour, 25 g/1 oz	100

Carrots   N

raw, 25 g/1 oz	6
old, boiled, 25 g/1 oz	5
medium carrot, 50 g/2 oz	12

Cashew nuts   N,P

25 g/1 oz	178

Cauliflower   N

raw, 25 g/1 oz	7
boiled, 25 g/1 oz	3

Celery   N

raw, 25 g/1 oz	2
boiled, 25 g/1 oz	1

Cheese   P

25 g/1 oz	
Brie	88
Camembert	88
Cheddar	120
Cheshire	110
cottage	30
cottage, low-fat	24
cream	125
curd	54
Danish blue	104

Edam	89
Feta	85
fromage frais, 8% fat	31
goat's cheese	87
Gorgonzola	111
Gouda, matured	110
Gruyère	131
Mozzarella	95
Parmesan	119
Parmesan, 15 ml tablespoon	30
quark, skimmed milk cheese, 25 g/1 oz	25
low-fat cheese, 25 g/1 oz	35
medium-fat cheese, 25 g/1 oz	50
Roquefort	100
soft, skimmed milk	25
Stilton	135
Wensleydale	115

Cherries   P
raw, 25 g/1 oz	13

Cherries, glacé
25 g/1 oz	60
cherries, glacé, one	10

Chestnuts   C
25 g/1 oz	49

Chicory   N
raw, 25 g/1 oz	3

Chinese leaves   N
25 g/1 oz	
raw	3
cooked	2

Chocolate
milk, 25 g/1 oz	167
plain, 25 g/1 oz	154
drinking, 5 ml teaspoon	10

Chutney, mango
15 ml tablespoon   40
Cider   P
dry, 300 ml/10 fl oz   100
Cocoa powder
25 g/1 oz   128
Coconut   N,P
desiccated, 25 g/1 oz   178
fresh, 25 g/1 oz   103
Corn on the cob   N,C
240 g/9 oz cob   170
frozen, each   180
Cornflour   C
25 g/1 oz   100
Courgettes   N
raw, 25 g/1 oz   3
each, 125 g/5 oz   15
Cranberries
25 g/1 oz   4
Cream   N
double, 25 g/1 oz   131
15 ml tablespoon   55
half cream, 15 ml tablespoon   20
single, 25 g/1 oz   62
15 ml tablespoon   30
soured, 25 g/1 oz   60
15 ml tablespoon   30
whipping, 25 g/1 oz   107
15 ml tablespoon   45
Crisps   C
25 g/1 oz   158
Crispbreads   C
cream crackers, each   31
oatcakes, each   60

Primula rye extra thin, per slice, crispbread	17	
Ryvita, per slice	25	
Ryking brown, per slice	35	
Scanda Brod crispbread, per slice	32	
Scanda Crisp crispbread, per slice	19	
water biscuits, each	32	
Cucumber		N
raw, 25 g/1 oz	3	
each	48	
Currants, black		P
raw, 25 g/1 oz	8	
Currants, red		P
raw, 25 g/1 oz	6	
Currants, white		P
raw, 25 g/1 oz	7	
Currants, dried		N,C
25 g/1 oz	69	
Damsons		P
raw, 25 g/1 oz	11	
Dandelion leaves		N
25 g/1 oz	9	
Dates		C
fresh, weighed with stones, 25 g/1 oz	60	
dates dried, 25 g/1 oz	74	
Eggs		
whole size 3	90	P
yolk size 3	65	N
white size 3	15	P
Endive		N
raw, 25 g/1 oz	3	
Fennel		
25 g/1 oz		N
raw	6	

boiled	8
Figs	N,C
raw, 25 g/1 oz	12
dried, 25 g/1 oz	60
per dried fig	30
Filo pastry	C
per sheet 33 gm	100
Flour	C
25 g/1 oz	
100% wholemeal	90
brown	93
white	96
Garlic	N
per clove	2
Ginger	
stem, in syrup, drained	
each piece	40
ground, 5 ml teaspoon	8
Ginger root	N
raw, peeled 25 g/1 oz	18
Gooseberries	P
ripe, 25 g/1 oz	10
Grapefruit	P
½ medium	18
juice, unsweetened, 25 g/1 oz	16
Grapes	C,[3]P
black or white, 25 g/1 oz	17
juice, unsweetened, 25 g/1 oz	19
Greengages	P
fresh, with stones, 25 g/1 oz	14
Hazelnuts	P,N
25 g/1 oz	108

[3]C if very sweet.

Herbs	N
chopped, fresh, 15 ml tablespoon	2
Honey	C
comb, 25 g/1 oz	80
clear or thick, 25 g/1 oz	82
per 5 ml teaspoon	20
Horseradish	N
raw, 25 g/1 oz	17
sauce, 15 ml tablespoon	13
Hummus	P
25 g/1 oz	100
Ice-cream	
25 g/1 oz	56
Jam	C
25 g/1 oz	74
per 5 ml teaspoon	15
Kiwi fruit	P
medium, each	30
Kumquat	P
25 g/1 oz	18
each	5
Leeks	N
raw 25 g/1 oz	9
boiled 25 g/1 oz	7
each	45
Lemons	P
each	12
curd 25 g/1 oz	86
juice 15 ml tablespoon	0
squash, 15 ml tablespoon	15
Lentils	P
dry, 25 g/1 oz	84
boiled, 25 g/1 oz	27

Lettuce		N
raw, 25 g/1 oz	3	
Limes		P
each	15	
cordial, 15 ml tablespoon	15	
juice, 15 ml tablespoon	0	
Liqueurs		C
25 g/1 oz	100	
Loganberries		P
fresh, 25 g/1 oz	5	
Lychees		P
each	8	
425 g/15 oz canned in syrup	150	
Mandarin oranges		P
medium whole fruit	20	
mandarins, canned, in juice, 25 g/1 oz	11	
Mangetout peas		N
25 g/1 oz	16	
Mango		P,C[4]
each	100	
fresh, 25 g/1 oz	17	
chutney, 15 ml tablespoon	40	C
canned fruit and syrup, 25 g/1 oz	22	C
Margarine		N
25 g/1 oz	225	
Marmalade		C
25 g/1 oz	74	
5 ml teaspoon	25	
Marmite		N
25 g/1 oz	51	
5 ml teaspoon	9	
Marrow		N
raw, 25 g/1 oz	3	

[4]C only if very ripe and sweet.

boiled, 25 g/1 oz	2
Mayonnaise	P
25 g/1 oz	202
Melon	N[5]
with skin, 25 g/1 oz	
cantaloupe	4
Charentais	4
Galia	6
honeydew	4
watermelon	3
Milk	P
dried, skimmed, 25 g/1 oz	92
fresh, skimmed, 300 ml/10 fl oz	90
fresh, semi-skimmed, 300 ml/10 fl oz	141
fresh, whole, 300 ml/10 fl oz	180
longlife, UHT, 300 ml/10 fl oz	180
soya, 300 ml/10 fl oz	100
Millet	C
25 g/1 oz	108
Mincemeat	
25 g/1 oz	36
Miso paste	N
25 g/1 oz	30
Molasses	C
25 g/1 oz	70
Mulberries	P
25 g/1 oz	10
Mushrooms	N
raw, 25 g/1 oz	2
fried, 25 g/1 oz	61
Mustard	N
25 g/1 oz	131
French, 5 ml teaspoon	10

[5]Does not combine well; best on its own.

Mustard and cress		N
25 g/1 oz	3	
Nectarines, each	50	P
Nuts		P,N
almonds, 25 g/1 oz	170	
Brazil, 25 g/1 oz	180	
hazel, 25 g/1 oz	108	
pistachios, 25 g/1 oz	166	
walnuts, 25 g/1 oz	156	
Oats		C
25 g/1 oz		
oats, rolled, uncooked	110	
oatmeal, dry	114	
Oils		N
average, 25 g/1 oz	250	
olive oil, 25 g/1 oz	263	
sesame oil, dark, 5 ml teaspoon	45	
oil, 15 ml tablespoon	140	
Olives		N
with stones, in brine, 25 g/1 oz	23	
olives, each	5	
Onions		N
raw, 25 g/1 oz	7	
boiled, 25 g/1 oz	4	
fried, 25 g/1 oz	100	
raw, whole medium	42	
Oranges		P
flesh only, 25 g/1 oz	10	
flesh with peel and pips, 25 g/1 oz	8	
each	50	
juice, 15 ml tablespoon	0	
squash, 15 ml tablespoon	15	
Parsnips		N
raw, 25 g/1 oz	14	

boiled, 25 g/1 oz	15
Passion fruit	P
each	10
Pasta	C
white, all types, dry, 25 g/1 oz	105
white, all types, cooked, 25 g/1 oz	33
wholemeal, dry, 25 g/1 oz	95
wholemeal, cooked, 25 g/1 oz	34
Pastry	C
25 g/1 oz	
flaky, raw	121
flaky, cooked	160
shortcrust, raw	129
shortcrust, cooked	149
Pawpaw	P,C[6]
fresh, 25 g/1 oz	11
each	100
Peaches	P
fresh, 25 g/1 oz	10
each	40
dried, raw, 25 g/1 oz	60
Peanuts	P[7]
25 g/1 oz	170
butter 25 g/1 oz	180
Pears	P,C[8]
eating, raw, 25 g/1 oz	9
cooking, raw, 25 g/1 oz	10
eating, each	50
Peas	N
fresh, raw, 25 g/1 oz	18
frozen, 25 g/1 oz	23

[6]C only if very ripe and sweet.
[7]Not recommended.
[8]C only if very ripe and sweet.

Pecans	P
25 g/1 oz	145
Peppers	N
fresh, 25 g/1 oz	9
red or green, each	20
Persimmon	P
fresh, 25 g/1 oz	17
Pickle	P
25 g/1 oz	30
15 ml tablespoon	15
Pineapple	P,N
fresh, 25 g/1 oz	13
juice, unsweetened, 25 g/1 oz	16
canned rings, each	26
Pistachio nuts	P,N
25 g/1 oz	166
Plums	P
fresh, 25 g/1 oz	10
stewed without sugar	6
Porridge oats	C
25 g/1 oz	115
Potatoes	C
crisps, 25 g/1 oz	158
new, boiled, 25 g/1 oz	21
old, baked in skins, 25 g/1 oz	24
old, boiled, 25 g/1 oz	23
potatoes, old, raw, 25 g/1 oz	24
Prunes	P
dried, dry, 25 g/1 oz	46
stewed without sugar,	
25 g/1 oz	23
Pumpkin	N
raw, 25 g/1 oz	4
seeds, 25 g/1 oz	155

Quark   P
  skimmed milk cheese,
  25 g/1 oz   25
  low-fat cheese, 25 g/1 oz   35
  medium-fat cheese, 25 g/1 oz   50
Radishes
  raw, 25 g/1 oz   4
Raisins   C,N
  dried, 25 g/1 oz   70
Raspberries   P
  25 g/1 oz   7
Rhubarb
  raw, 25 g/1 oz   2
Rice   C
  brown or white, dry, 25 g/1 oz   102
  boiled, 25 g/1 oz   35
Salad cream
  15 ml tablespoon   50
Salsify   N
  boiled, 25 g/1 oz   5
Semolina   C
  25 g/1 oz   100
Sesame   N,P
  oil, dark, 5 ml teaspoon   45
  seeds, 25 g/1 oz   160
  cream, tahini, 5 ml teaspoon   N,P
Sherry   P
  dry, small glass   60
Soy sauce   N
  25 g/1 oz   20
  15 ml tablespoon   10
Soya flour   P
  full-fat, 25 g/1 oz   127
  low-fat, 25 g/1 oz   100

Soya milk		P
300 ml/10 fl oz	100	
Spinach		N
raw, 25 g/1 oz	4	
boiled, 25 g/1 oz	7	
frozen, 25 g/1 oz	8	
Spring onions		N
25 g/1 oz	10	
each	4	
Sprouted beans		P
25 g/1 oz	28	
Stock powder		N
vegetarian, 25 g/1 oz	6	
Strawberries		P
fresh, 25 g/1 oz	7	
Sugar		C
25 g/1 oz	112	
Sunflower seeds		P,N
25 g/1 oz	170	
Swedes		N
raw, 25 g/1 oz	6	
boiled, 25 g/1 oz	5	
Sweet potato		C
boiled, 25 g/1 oz	23	
Sweetcorn		C
fresh, 25 g/1 oz	28	
frozen, 25 g/1 oz	25	
Sweets		C[9]
boiled sweets, 25 g/1 oz	93	
chocolate, milk	167	
chocolate, plain	154	
chocolates, fancy	132	
fruit gums	48	

[9] C, but not recommended.

liquorice allsorts	89
peppermints	111
popcorn, cooked, no sugar	32
toffee, homemade	113
Bounty bar	136
Mars bar, standard-size bar	290
Syrup	C[10]
golden, 25 g/1 oz	84
Tangerines	P
with skin and pips, 25 g/1 oz	7
Tartex	P
25 g/1 oz	68
Tofu	P
firm, 25 g/1 oz	15
silken, 25 g/1 oz	16
Tomatoes	N
raw, 25 g/1 oz	4
canned, 25 g/1 oz	4
dried, 25 g/1 oz	12
each	12
juice unsweetened, 25 g/1 oz	6
ketchup, 25 g/1 oz	35
purée, 25 g/1 oz	19
Treacle	C
black, 25 g/1 oz	72
Turnip	N
raw, 25 g/1 oz	5
boiled, 25 g/1 oz	3
Vegetable juice	N
unsweetened, 25 g/1 oz	6
Vinegar	P
25 g/1 oz	1

[10]C, but not recommended.

Walnuts		P,N
shelled, 25 g/1 oz	156	
walnut half	15	
Watercress		N
raw, 25 g/1 oz	4	
Watermelon		P[11]
with skin, 25 g/1 oz	5	
Wheatgerm		N
15 ml tablespoon	30	
Wine		P
dry white, 125 ml/4 fl oz	75	
dry red, 125 ml/4 fl oz	80	
Yeast		N
dried, 25 g/1 oz	50	
fresh, 25 g/1 oz	15	
Yeast extract		N
25 g/1 oz	50	
5 ml teaspoon	10	
Yogurt		P
low-fat, unflavoured, 25 g/1 oz	15	
sheep's, Greek, 25 g/1 oz	26	
whole-milk, unflavoured, 25 g/1 oz	20	
fruit-flavoured, average, 25 g/1 oz	22	

[11]Best eaten alone.

Afterword

In this book I have touched on many different ideas that relate to the way we feel about our bodies, our emotions and our lives. I have discussed the value of a vegetarian way of life for getting slim and staying slim, given a choice of practical, effective diets, some delicious new recipes and many tips. I hope you have found it all helpful and inspiring. I believe strongly that we have a far greater ability to create the lives we want than most people realise. I would like to see us all with the power to direct our thoughts in a positive way, to enjoy our emotions but not to be ruled by them, to flow with the impulse of life and to get in touch with our inner power, joy and love.

Further Reading

Beeken, Jenny, *Yoga of the Heart*, The White Eagle Publishing Trust, 1990

Birkinshaw, Elsye, *Think Slim, Be Slim*, Thorsons, 1984

Davis, Patricia, *Aromatherapy An A-Z*, The C.W. Daniel Company Ltd, 1990

De Bairacli Levy, Juliette, *The Illustrated Herbal Handbook*, Faber, 1982

Dicken, Anna, *A Woman in Your Own Right*, Quartet, 1982

Elliot, Rose, *Rose Elliot's Mother and Baby Book*, Fontana, 1989; *The Green Age Diet*, Fontana, 1990

Gawain, Shakti, and King, Laurel, *Living in the Light*, Eden Grove Publications, 1988; *Creative Visualisation*, Bantam, 1987

Gimbel, Theo, DCE, *Healing Through Colour*, The C.W. Daniel Company Ltd, 1987

Grant, Doris, and Joice, Jean, *Don't Mix Foods Which Fight*, Thorsons, 1984

Griggs, Barbara, *The Home Herbal*, Pan, 1986

Hay, Louise L., *You Can Heal Your Life*, Eden Grove Publications, 1988

Hoare, Sophy, *Yoga*, Macdonald Guidelines, 1977

Howard, Judy, *The Bach Flower Remedies Step by Step*, The C.W. Daniel Company Ltd, 1990

Jampolsky, Gerald, G., *Love is Letting Go of Fear*, Celestial Arts, US, 1982

Keyes, Ken, *A Conscious Person's Guide to Relationships*, Living Love Publications, 1985; *The Handbook to Higher Consciousness*, Living Love Publications, 1985

LeShan, Laurence, *How to Meditate – A Guide to Self-Discovery*, Crucible, 1989

Lowen, Alexander, *Bioenergetics*, Penguin Books, 1979; *The Way to Vibrant Health – a Manual of Bioenergetic Exercise*, Harper and Row, New York, 1977

Moscovitz, Judy, *The Rice Diet Report*, Bantam, New York, 1988

Ray, Sondra, *Loving Relationships*, Celestial Arts, US, 1984

Rodegast, Pat and Stanton, Judith, *Emmanuel's Book*, Bantam, 1987

Scott Peck, M., *The Road Less Travelled*, Arrow, 1990

Vaughan, Frances, *The Inward Arc*, New Science Library, 1986

Verner-Bonds, Lilian, *The Healing Rainbow* (cassette tape), Astro Associates, 137 Hendon Lane, London N3 3PR

Wall, Vicky, *The Miracle of Colour Healing*, The Aquarian Press, 1990

Addresses

The Edward Bach Centre, Mount Vernon, Sotwell, Wallingford, Oxon. OX10 OPZ

The London School of Aromatherapy, P.O. Box 780, London NW5 1DY.
Send 9½ × 6½ s.a.e. for prospectus of courses, and for a list of trained aromatherapists in the British Isles and other countries.

For high quality aromatherapy oils:

Bodytreats Ltd, 15 Approach Road, Raynes Park, London SW20 8BA

Fragrant Earth, P.O. Box 182, Taunton, Somerset TA1 3SD

Norman and Germaine Rich, 2 Coval Gardens, London SW14 7DG

For an astrological personality profile, which can be very helpful in understanding yourself and your potential better, send your name, details of your date and place of birth and £12.50 to Rose Elliot Horoscopes, PO Box 16, Eastleigh, Hampshire SO5 5YP.

Subject Index

Recipe Index

❦